GENEALOGICAL RECORDS AND TRADITIONAL KNOWLEDGE SYSTEM

GENEALOGICAL RECORDS AND TRADITIONAL KNOWLEDGE SYSTEM

Study in Four Sacred Centres of India

Editor

Kakali Chakrabarty

Anthropological Survey of India
Government of India
Kolkata

ISBN: 978-81-212-1273-1

Price: ₹ 550

First Published 2015

Published by

Gyan Publishing House
23, Main Ansari Road, Daryaganj,
New Delhi - 110002
Phones : 23282060, 23261060
Fax : (011) 23285914
E-mail: books@gyanbooks.com
website: gyanbooks.com

Laser Typesetting: Rajender Vashist, Delhi.

Printed at: G. Print Process, Delhi.

Cataloging in Publication Data--DK
Courtesy: D.K. Agencies (P) Ltd. <docinfo@dkagencies.com>

Genealogical records and traditional knowledge system : study in four sacred centres of India / editor, Kakali Chakrabarty.

p. cm.
Contributed articles.
Includes bibliographical references and index.
ISBN 9788121212731

1. Hindu pilgrims and pilgrimages--India. 2. Temple records and registers--India. 3. Ethnoscience--India. 4. India--Genealogy. I. Chakrabarty, Kakali.

DDC 294.5350954 23

Contents

Foreword

The present volume is the outcome of a National Project, namely "People of India: Cultural Diversity: Tangible and Intangible Cultural Heritage (Traditional Knowledge)" undertaken by the Anthropological Survey of India during the 11th Five Year Plan period (2008-2012). A number of research arenas were selected under this project focussing on the traditional knowledge system of the contemporary societies, including the tribes of India. One of the arenas was to collect the genealogical records of the pilgrims of various Indian temples. It was still a virgin field and was a challenge for the researchers as the situation was not known fully. The Anthropological Survey of India decided to step into this maiden arena and our experienced researchers with their competence did excellent work in this area.

The study revealed that *jajmani* relation was the foundation of development of this precise knowledge system. The system survived over centuries and remained almost unchanged through different politico-historical periods. Initially it was perhaps the intention of the kings and feudal lords to understand and evaluate the extent of popularity of the deities and shrines under their control. All these temples were under the patronage of the then ruling families of the region. Our researchers came out with very rich empirical information through detailed interviews and analysed the same in an organised manner. As the system is embodied in the temple activities as a whole, the socio-religious significance of the particular holy centre in relation to the pan-Indian scenario has also been discussed. This added further importance to the studies.

The present volume is an important contribution to the study of pilgrimage in India. It opened up a new vista of understanding the significance of the sacred centre in the cultural tradition of India. I am confident that it would be useful for further exploring into different aspects of this very unique traditional knowledge system by the social scientists, historians and students of Indian religions.

Kolkata
18th April, 2013

Prof K.K. Misra
Director
Anthropological Survey of India

Editor's Note

The present volume explores a maiden field of Anthropological research that is the traditional knowledge system through the records on pilgrims by the temple priests over centuries. The work is a part of the 11th five year plan project (2008-2012) of the Anthropological Survey of India focusing on cultural diversity and traditional knowledge of Indian populations. This part of the project was originally conceived for the single situation of Jagannath temple in the state of Odisha but later on extended to three more situations in other parts of the country. These additional three areas of study included three famous sacred centres namely Haridwar or Hardwar in the state of Uttar Pradesh, Kamakhya/ (Kamakshya) in the state of Assam and Rameswaram in the state of Tamil Nadu. There are many more important sacred centers in India which may have similar kind of knowledge system in practice but to delimit the study four situations were finally identified.

In its simplest term traditional knowledge is perceived as knowledge, which is collectively held from experience and transmitted over generations within the community boundary. Some of this knowledge remains secret to their custodians, while many other forms of knowledge are expressed in public domain and shared within and beyond the boundary of the community. It is generally transmitted orally and the conservation ethics are often part of traditional knowledge. No single definition is enough to explain the diverse forms of knowledge system of a community or a population.

Kamal K. Misra (2005:4) preferred the term 'Indigenous Knowledge' in describing traditional knowledge. According to him indigenous knowledge is local and culture-specific; it is orally transmitted through imitation and demonstration; it is the consequence of practical engagement in every life and is constantly reinforced by experience, trial and error and deliberate experiment; it tends to be empirical and empirico-hypothetical rather theoretical in the strict sense; it is people's science, and is asymmetrically distributed in a population; the organisation of indigenous knowledge is essentially functional, denotative know-how geared to practical response and performance; and it is holistic, integrative and situated within broader culture traditions. Traditional knowledge has been conceived by him as essentially community specific, restricted within the community and is accumulated through age long interaction with the immediate environment. Such knowledge remains secret to their custodians, conserved and maintained over generations. According to the World intellectual Property Organisation document, 'local communities justly cherish traditional knowledge (TK) as a part of their very cultural identities.' For many communities, traditional knowledg forms part of a holistic world-view, and is inseparable from their very ways of life and their culture, values, spiritual beliefs and customary legal systems. This means that it is vital to sustain not merely the knowledge but the social and physical environment of which it forms an integral part. Traditional knowledge and indigenous knowledge are often used as synonyms. However, indigenous knowledge is more confined to a group or locality, while traditional knowledge can be indigenous or non-indigenous for the practicing community.

In Indian cultural tradition pilgrimage is an essential part of one's spiritual activities. There are innumerable holy places centering round the temples, rivers, mountains, sea and each being traced from mythological divinity. The stories are traced from the great epics of *Ramayana* and *Mahabharata*, the ancient sacred scriptures of *Upanisada* or *Puranas* and so on. In almost all the great temples there is a tradition of keeping records of the pilgrims while they come on pilgrimage. Maintaining of records is very much a part and parcel of the temple activities. Interestingly these records, named differently in different areas, are maintained over centuries and are still continuing as a living tradition. The very survival of the system through centuries speaks of the immense importance of the tradition.

The present project probes into the system in four of the major sacred centres to understand the traditional knowledge involved in this process. Let me explain why we have identified these records with the genealogical records? It is of course a methodological term commonly in use within Anthropology. Genealogy simply means pedigree or the study of pedigrees, i.e., descent traced continuously from ancestors. In these temples records, the information about the pilgrims were maintained over generations and family wise, often the records of a particular lineage or a family were maintained by a particular priest and after his demise the records were being kept on by his descent in a process of continuous interaction between the priest's and the pilgrim's descending generations through a kind of religious bonding often identical with the *jajmani* system of ancient Indian society.

In Indian society pilgrimage is an important aspect in one's religious performances and it is a common intention to visit a sacred centre on repeated occasions. Therefore the same individual interacts with the same priest on more than one occasion and gets religious service from him. Repeated interaction makes the records updated. Such relationship between the priests and the devotees often continues over generations from both ends and so the records continue to be updated over generations. In course of time it takes a shape of genealogical records with updating of the information time to time or in other words, anybody can draw a family tree or pedigree for a particular family from these informations. Let me cite an example from the Odisha situation.

Following chart shows the method of keeping record of a pilgrim:

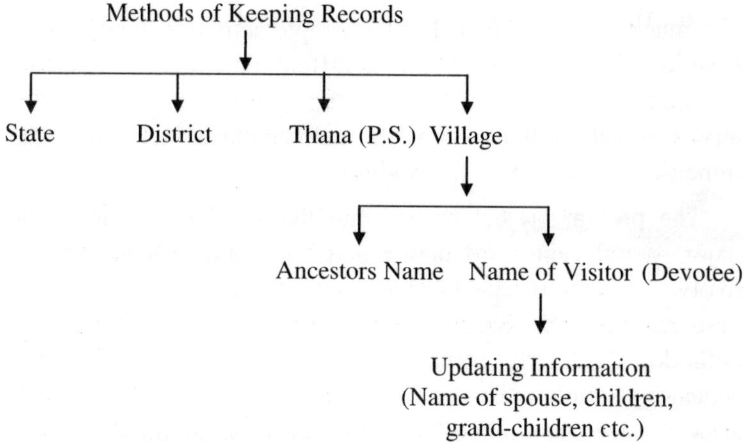

Interestingly all the four studies exhibited almost identical method of recording the information though they are wide apart in terms of geographical location. The records are maintained by the priest or a group of temple servitors at different capacity. Such records are called differently in different temples. In Jagannath temple it is called *Warja* or *Warija* while in Kamakhya temple or in Haridwar it is popular as *banshabali*. The present volume included four articles covering four sacred centres in India, dedicated to four prime deities under Hindu doctrine. Each of these sacred centres has mythological significance and attracts huge pilgrimage from all over India.

According to Hinduism, the very basic idea behind pilgrimage is the salvation of soul. Human's earthly activities are guided by the concept of *papa*, the sin and *punya*, the virtue. Through pilgrimage one can achieve *punya*, the ultimate result of which is to attend the salvation or *mukti* from sin. Under the Hindu doctrine the ultimate aim of spiritual function is to attain *moksha*, the final emancipation of soul. Our researchers came across such philosophical ideologies through their interactions with the people in respective fields. Thus, Kamakhya, the *Sati pitha* or *Shakti pitha*, Jagannath temple, the *bhojan kshetra* of Lord Vishnu/ Krishna, Haridwar, the gateway to the land of Lord Siva or Lord

Vishnu, Rameswaram, the site of Jyotirlingam play a significant role in the Hindu religion.

In religious sphere, priest occupies an important place. He mediates between a devotee and the deity. In Hindu religion a Brahmin serves as priest. Therefore any devotee or pilgrim requires the service of a Brahman to offer worship to the deity. The priest acts as the bodily representative of God, the supernatural being. Such interaction between the priest and the devotee is the very basis of the development of *jajmani* relations in all the four situations under study.

Jagannath temple in Odisha is one of four *dham* (holy place) under the sect of Vaishnavism. The study on Jagannath temple found the *jajmani* system as the strength of this tradition of *warja.* Interestingly the system is maintained in the same method as it was in ancient times. During the olden days palm leaves were in use for writing and most of the state offices have such palm-leave record books in their *warja* library. Maintenance of *warja* is a part of the temple services and a group of Pandās, especially the Pratihari Pandās were assigned with the job. The duties were allotted during the days of king's ruling in pre-British era and are still continuing without any change, over centuries.

The study focused on the traditional knowledge system involved in *warja.* We must consider the fact that the age-old method of indexing of the records in Jagannath temple is very much similar to the modern technique of indexing as followed in modern libraries while this was developed and practiced by the Pandās since ancient times. The administration of Jagannath temple was always run by the kings and the rulers whosoever was in power. The system of offering services was introduced by the Hindu kings in ancient times and a group of servitors to the deities, called *sevakas*, were appointed. There were about one hundred and nineteen services categories in the temple each of which was hereditary in character and succeeded from one generation to another through male line of descend, i.e., from father to son and so on. The servitor or *Sebaka* system is a men's domain strictly and women have no role to play. The system continued unchanged through different historical times even through the British period. After Independence of the country the Government of Odisha assumed control over the temple but the system remained unchanged.

Warja in the Jagannath temple is maintained by a number of Pandā families through an institutional system called state offices in local usage, each of which is headed by a Pandā (Brahmin servitor of the temple of Lord Jagannath). Each State office has a jurisdiction of working area. The present proprietors are actually the male-line descendents of the founder Pandās who were assigned with such job during the king's days in pre-British era. The state offices are mostly named after the founder Pandā who served as guru, the religious teacher, for the *jajmans* or the devotees. That network of *jajmani* relationship has been inherited by the present proprietors since ancient times and maintaining the old records of the *jajmans* in a systematic method. Therefore from their records any of the jajman can draw a family tree for his family or lineage. Until very recent times these records were submitted to the court of law for establishing one's claim on family property. Our researchers find the *Warja* tradition in Jagannath temple is a well organised system that is surviving with its own strength through centuries.

The Rameshwar temple at Rameswaram in Tamil Nadu attracts devout pilgrims from all parts of India. It earned the sanctity of a holy city and a major centre of pilgrimage for the Hindu Saivaites from one of the shrines of Jyotirlingam. A Jyotirlingam or Jyotirlinga is a shrine where lord Siva, one of the great God of Hindu faith, is worshipped in the form of a Jyotirlingam, i.e., the pillar of light (Jyoti=light; lingam=pillar). It is believed that lord Siva first manifested himself in the form of a Jyotirlinga. There are twelve Jyotirlinga in India, located at different corners of the country. Each of the twelve Jyotirlinga sites is named after its presiding deity, each considered as the different manifestation of lord Siva. Besides Rameswaram the other Jyotirlingas are Somnath in Gujarat, Mallikarjuna at Srisailam in Andhra Pradesh, Mahakaleswar at Ujjain in Madhya Pradesh, Omkareshwar in Madhya Pradesh, Kedarnath in Himalayas, Bhimashankar in

Maharashtra, Viswanath in Varanasi, Triambakeshwar in Maharashtra, Vaidyanath Jyotirlinga at Deoghar in Jharkhand, Nageswar at Dwarka in Gujarat and Ghushmeshwar at Shiwar in Rajasthan.

The significance of the Rameshwar temple is traced from the great epic of *Ramayana*. It is believed that Rama, the central figure of the epic *Ramayana* who is considered as the form of Lord Vishnu, worshipped and appeased Lord Siva at this place. The place is also known as holy Kashi after the great sacred centre of Kashi of Benaras in the State of Uttar Pradesh. According to Hindu religious belief if one dies at Kashi (U.P.) his soul achieves *mukti,*i.e., ultimate salvation. In case of Rameswaram it is believed that only by a *darsana* (the holy sight) of the temple one achieves *mukti* and gets relieved from all kinds of sin. Our study found Rameswaram as a symbol of national unity; spiritually it unites the Saivaites and Vaishnavites.

Rameswaram as a sacred centre receives pilgrims from the neighbouring countries of Sri-Lanka and Nepal also. The devotees come mainly for the worship of Siva as well as for the ancestral worship. The local people visit the temple on the occasion of *rites de passage*. Temple records are maintained for the devotees or pilgrims by the priest group who were brought from the ancient Maharashtra by the then rulers of Rameswaram. The method of recording information is almost similar to that of other centres under the present study. The priest maintains a family register and updates it time to time as and when the members of the same family/lineage make a visit again to the temple. Today, the records system plays an important role in the field of settling legal cases regarding inheritance or property disputes. The study probed into the historicity and development of the religious centre as well.

Hardwar, also called Haridwar, is another ancient pilgrimage centre which traces its significance from both Saivism and Vaisnavism. The religious importance of Hardwar also lies in the practice of ancestral worship under the Hindu doctrine. Taking advantage of its geographical location the place is regarded as the gateway to the sacred centres in the Himalayan range. Being situated on the bank of River Ganga, the holy river of mythological origin, Hardwar attracts pilgrimage for its temple deities as well as for the river Ganga who is appeased as a deity. The place offers religious salvation for the devotees. A holy dip into the river Ganga relieves from all sins. The sanctity of Hardwar is also referred to by the sacred scripture of *Purana* and *Mahabharata*. Historicity of the town is traceable from the earlier accounts of Hiuen Tsang (629-645 A.D.), the early Muslim chroniclers, Abu Rihan and Rashid-ud-din and of Abul Fazl during the reign of Akbar (1556-1605 A.D.) and so on. In the study of Hardwar our researcher found a strong bond of *Jajmani* relationship between the priests and the devotees/pilgrims. The records of the pilgrims are maintained by the priests in their own way and the method of recording is interestingly similar to our other studies. The tradition is still surviving. Unlike Jagannath temple, in Hardwar such records are maintained by two groups of priests: *Thirth Purohit* and *Maha Brahman*; the former serves the higher caste people while the later serves the lowly ranked castes, mostly the scheduled castes. Both groups follow the same method of recording.

The fourth situation, the Kamakhya temple of Assam reveres the mother-cult, the *Sakti Pitha* (the seat of Sakti or mother cult), typical to the eastern part of India. The importance of Kamakhya temple has its root in the sacred scripture of *Purana*. It recognises Kamakhya as one of the 51 *Sakti-pithas,* i.e., mother-cult centres in India.

In the Kamakhya Temple genealogical records, as have been designated by us, are called *banshabali* in local usage. The records are maintained by Brahmin priests who are commonly known as Pandā as well as Bardeori and Nandeori. The record book is locally known as *Jatrik Khata* (*Jatri* denotes pilgrims/ devotees). This particular sacred centre is actually a cluster of temples, each having a presiding god or goddess, constructed around the main temple of Kamakhya. The Brahmins who have been worshipping the goddess Kamakhya are called Bardeoris and the Brahmins who have been worshipping other residing deities around the Kamakhya Temple are called Nandeori.

The *Jatrik Khatas* or record books are of two types: one is entry book and the other is copy book where finally the information is noted down by the recorder in his own way which is to be updated from time to time. *Jajmani* relation is the basic strength of this tradition alike to other situations under this study. Pandās are the Tirtha Gurus, the religious teacher for the pilgrims. From him the devotees learn about the significance of the temple of Kamakhya, about the divinity of Gods and Goddesses at the sacred complex. Our study also probed into the recent changes in the *jajmani* relation and observed that the system is gradually losing its importance in the present social scenario.

All the studies are based on empirical data. A guideline was prepared by the Anthropological Survey of India for the National project on Traditional Knowledge through threadbearing exercise. A part of the guideline was applicable to the present studies and that has been taken into use.

Through this maiden venture, Anthropological Survey of India has made a footmark in this interesting field of knowledge which opens up a new vista to the anthropological society for further queries and updating the knowledge. The contributors deserve appreciation that with their finer competence in the discipline and hard work they were able to bring out the uniqueness of each situation successfully and unearthed the traditional knowledge and insight towards the subject.

The success story of any research work stands on encouragement, cooperation and academic as well as administrative support from different personalities at different capacities. None of these supports is comparable to each other as each in its own perspective is great to the researchers. Starting from the very inception of the project till the publication of this volume, sincere efforts and cooperation from different corners were involved. I express sincere gratitude to all whoever has extended any kind of cooperation at any point of time in relation to this project.

Kakali Chakrabarty

List of Contributors

Basu, Krishna, Research Associate (Cultural), Anthropological Survey of India, Eastern Regional Centre, EN 79, Sector V, Salt Lake, Kolkata 700 091, e-mail: krishna.basu@hotmail.com

Chakrabarty, Kakali, Anthropological Survey of India, Eastern Regional Centre, EN 79, Sector V, Salt Lake, Kolkata 700 091. e-mail: kchakrabartyansi@yahoo.in

Mandal, Krishna, Anthropological Survey of India, Eastern Regional Centre, EN 79, Sector V, Salt Lake, Kolkata 700 091, e-mail: kmandal010@gmail.com

Sinha Roy, K.M., Anthropological Survey of India, Sub Regional Centre, Jagdalpur, Dharampura No. 1, Chhattisgarh, e-mail: sinharoykm@gmail.com

1

Warja and the Traditional Knowledge System: A Study in Jagannath Temple of Puri

Kakali Chakrabarty, Krishna Mandal and ***K.M. Sinha Roy***

In India, pilgrimage is an obvious part of the Hindu religious life. It is believed that one has to make pilgrimage to at least *char dham,* i.e., four sacred centre (*char*=four, *dham*=sacred centre) to earn salvation of life. The virtue earned of the pilgrimages will be carried forward to one's succeeding life after death (Hindu philosophy believes in rebirth of soul and therefore life is a continuous process of birth and rebirth of one's soul). Therefore, one can easily assume the immense importance of pilgrimage in one's lifetime. The four sacred centers would be chosen according to one's particular sect of doctrine. In Hindu religion there are different sects named according to their worshipping God or Goddess who happened to be one of the major figure of the Hindu religious order, like the Vaishnava, i.e., the worshippers of Vishnu, the Saiva, i.e., the worshippers of Siva, the Sakta or the worshippers of Sakti, the cult of energy in the form of female figure (as of a deity) and many others. The concept of *dham* developed around the temples of different deities is full of myths, legends and stories. In India almost all the great temples earned a reputation as a *dham* with the support of some or other kind of myths and legends and attract pilgrims from some or other sect of doctrines.

It was a common practice for almost all these great temples to maintain the records of the pilgrims as a part of their organisational system. Such records were not only preserved over generations but also updated from time to time with the information of the descending generations. This was possible because of the regular interaction of the priests and the devotees, the *Bhaktas* through generations. As a consequence of this kind of interactions over generations, there developed a well organised documentation system that generated huge information about the descent of the family and lineage of the pilgrims. In course of time these accumulated information about any particular lineage or family over generations has taken a shape of genealogical records of the pilgrims. The practice gradually produced a systematic and precise knowledge of recording, preservation and maintenance of such documents, thereby developed a traditional knowledge pool.

The famous Jagannath temple, located in the coastal town of Puri in Odisha, a State in the eastern part of India, is one of the great temples of Vaishnava tradition that maintains such genealogical records of the pilgrims. The tradition started under the patronage of the kings centuries ago and continued as a living practice till date. The records are traditionally maintained by a group of Pandās (the Brahman servitors to the deity) of the Jagannath temple. In their own usage these genealogical records are called *warja*.

The present study traces the origin and development of such traditional knowledge system associated with *warja*. The knowledge of *warja* is continuing over generations through oral traditions, training and socialisation process. The importance of this tradition lies in its antiquity and massiveness of stored data. The tradition has a religious overtone which implies its immense importance to the great mass of Indian population.

Methodology: Tools and Techniques

Standard Anthropological methods and techniques were used for data collection. The major tools used were interview, observation and case study methods. Besides, household census schedule and open end questionnaire were used for generating both qualitative and quantitative information. Published literary resources were explored from both personal and library collections. Audio-visual recording formed another major resource of information. All the methods principally followed a guideline, focusing on the traditional knowledge system. Key resource personnel included local researchers, temple office bearers, temple priests and local elites.

The *Warja*: The Records

The term *warja* literally means archival items. Some also call it *warija*. *Warija* is the local word for a note or a diary. For a Pandā *warja* and *warija* means records, which in fact are records of information about the pilgrims over generations. It has been observed that the term *warja* though is a common connotation for the Pandās associated with the tradition but is not very popular to the common people in general. It is an age old system involving the temple organisation and the devotees or the pilgrims, commonly referred to as *Bhakta* or *Jatri*. It is important to note here that *warja* is the outcome of the traditional *jajmani* relationship between the Pandā and the *Bhakta*. In any institutionalised religious centre of the great Hindu tradition a person or a devotee cannot approach the God or the Supreme divinity directly by himself. To offer *puja* (worship) one needs the help of a priest who acts as a mediator between the God and the devotee or sometimes he acts on behalf of the supreme beings. Therefore, for a pilgrim the role of a priest is important. To make a pilgrimage the *Bhakta* should approach through a priest (Pandā). Here the *jajmani* relationship works and such relationship formed the very basis of the *warja* tradition.

It is too difficult to bring out the actual date of origin of the *warja* tradition but people trace the very system as old as of the temple of Puri. It may be taken into account that *warja* tradition is a part of the total system of the temple activities and therefore it can be understood only in relation to the total activities of the Temple. A well organised knowledge system is involved from the collection of information to its preservation and maintenance.

According to the Pandās, maintaining *warja* is a way of service to the God; service to the God is called *seba* in the temple usage and the person who performs *seba* is called *Sebaka*. For a *Sebaka, seba* is his hereditary right. Each of these Pandās has hereditary *seva* to the God and maintaining *warja* is an additional duty for them through which they earned further opportunity to offer their services to the Lord. Presently recording and maintenance of *warja* has been largely institutionalised that operates through formal officiating bodies, commonly referred to as state-office. Each of such state-office is run by a particular Pandā lineage. This aspect will be discussed later in more details.

The following diagram attempted to show the way this traditional knowledge system works.

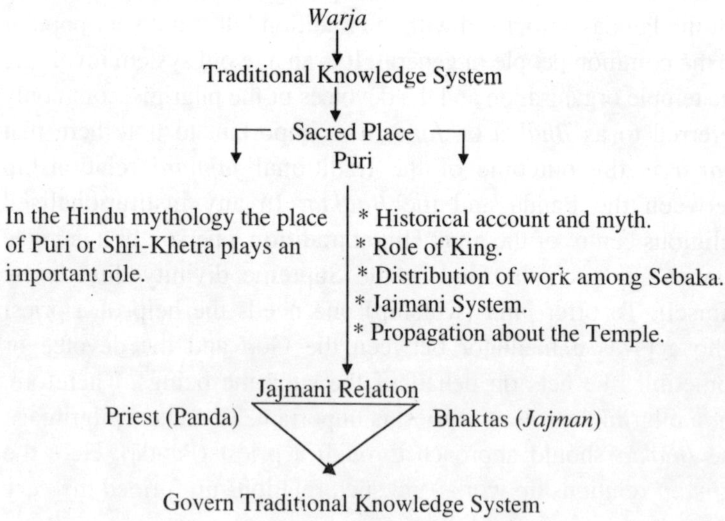

Fig. 1.

Historicity and Religious Significance of the Jagannath Temple and the Town of Puri

Puri, the coastal town of Odisha is regarded as a holy place of Hindu pilgrimage since long historical past. The place earned its holiness because of the famous Hindu temple enshrined Lord Jagannath. The temple occupies central position to the life and tradition of Puri and therefore the culture and tradition of the people of Puri necessarily has a religious overtone. The name Jagannath (Lord of the Universe) is a combination of the Sanskrit words *Jagat* (Universe) and *Nath* (Lord). The temple is an important pilgrimage destination for many Hindu traditions, particularly for the worshippers of Lord Vishnu and Krishna, i.e., the Vaishnava tradition of the Hindu pantheon. Here Jagannath represents Lord Vishnu or Krishna, the forms of *Purusottama*, the Lord of the Lords. According to the Pandās the place is one and the foremost of *Chār Dhām* for Vaishnavas and therefore forms an important centre for pilgrimages that must be visited at least once in one's lifetime. The four *dham* are located in four directions, one each in north, south, east and western part of the country, each meant for specific function of the Lord Vishnu. In northern India there is Badrinath *dham*, believed to be the *tapa-kshetra*, the place of meditation and religious austerities of Lord Vishnu (*tapa*=religious austerity, *kshetra*=place). In the west there is Dwarka *dham*, the capital of the Lord's kingdom, a place meant for *Rajbesa,* his kingly adornment.

Rameswaram in the south is his *sayan-kshetra*, the place for taking rest for the Lord and Puri in the east is regarded as *bhojan-kshetra*, the place of dinning (*bhojan*=eating) of Mahaprabhu, the great Master (*maha*=great, *Prabhu*=the master; Mahaprabhu here denotes the lord Jagannath). Puri is also known as *anna-kshetra* (*anna* literally means cooked rice) as *anna* is the prime item of offering to the Lord. Being the *bhojan-kshetra* or *anna-kshetra* for the Lord offering *bhoga* (food for the god) especially the *anna-bhoga* (food with cooked rice) is pivotal to the worship at Jagannath temple and *seba* or ritual services to the God is rendered through offering of food time to time. To be precise worship is performed in the form of offering food only and the temple has an elaborate system of *bhoga-seba* to the deity, organised around the offering of food. It is believed that pilgrimage to the Jagannath *dham* and eating *prasada* (generally called *mahaprasada*), the leftover of god's food, earn the final salvation of life for a devotee and make him or her free from the burden of bearing another mortal life through rebirth. In their own word '*sab tirtha bār bār Puri tirtha ekbār*' meaning all places of pilgrimage (*tirtha*=a place of pilgrimage) required to visit on more occasions but only one visit to Puri *tirtha* will earn salvation to one's life.

Being a major sacred centre the temple of Puri attracts pilgrims from all over the country from very early days. Puri also houses one of the four great *Matha* (Hindu Monasteries) founded by Adi Sankaracharya (788CE-820CE), a theologian of Hinduism and the greatest exponent of Advaita Vedanta philosophy. His other three Mathas are located at Sringeri in the state of Karnataka in south India, Dwarka in the state of Gujarat in western part of India and Jyotirmath (Joshimath) in the state of Uttarakhand in north India. Ramananda, a 14th century religious leader and a follower of Ramanuja, the Sri Vaishnava religious leader, was also associated with the temple of Jagannath. In later days a number of *Mathas* were established by different religious teachers (*guru*) each of which had definite *seba* to the temple (see appendix). *Mathas* were also involved in various rituals on different festive occasions. In return they used to receive the share of *prasāda* (food after being ritually offered to the deity becomes *prasāda*) and other facilities from the temple for instance a room in the temple kitchen premises, *khadua pata* (silken cloth) etc.

Till date the *Mathas* receive the respective share of food from the temple kitchen (*Rasashālā* or *Rasa*). The major *Mathas* enjoy a place in the temple kitchen and maintain their own hearth. Such kitchens are named after the particular *Matha* it works for e.g. Emār *Rasa* (named after Emar *Matha*), Bada Oriya *Rasa* (named after Bada Oriya *Matha*), Uttar Parsa *Rasa* (named after Uttar Parsa *Matha*), Raghab Das *Rasa* (named after Raghab

Das *Matha*) and so forth. The Supakar or Suār performs the job of cooking for them. Suār is a category of *Sebaka* who are traditionally trusted with the job of cooking in the temple kitchen.

In the olden days of king's ruling *Mathas* used to receive patronage from the Raja, the king of Puri. Presently many of the *Mathas* are facing severe economic crisis as there is no such patronage for them and therefore the assigned *seba* to Lord Jagannath are often not maintained by them properly. However, they attend the festivities of the temple. Puri is also of particular significance to the followers of Gaudiya Vaishnavism, the founder of whom Sri Chaitanya Mahaprabhu (1485-1527), the great religious reformist and the profounder of Vaishnavism in 15th-16th centuries Bengal attracted to lord Jagannath and devoted the later part of his life to the worship of Jagannath at Puri. He popularised the worship of Jagannath.

According to the Odisha State Gazetteer (1990, p. 11), Shri Chaitanya came to Odisha in 1509 A.D. Presently there is one Gouriya *Matha* at Puri dedicated to the worship of Sri Chaitanya but it does not have any direct socio-religious bearing to the temple of Lord Jagannath. O'Mally (re 2007: 96) observed that 'the doctrines of Chaitanya found ready acceptance among the Oriyās, by whom he is regarded as an incarnation of Krishna and Radha adoration of Chaitanya has become a sort of family worship throughout Odisha' as he quoted from Sir W.W. Hunter (*ibid*, 96).

The reference of Jagannath and Purusottam *kshetra* are found since the beginning of 8th century A.D. (Odisha State Gazetteer, 1990, p. 12). There are a number of theoretical propositions regarding the origin of Lord Jagannath by various scholars. The most popular belief goes with the tribal origin of the deity. The legend (see appendix) says that Jagannath was originally a worshipping deity of the Sabara Raja (the chieftain of Sabara tribe of Odisha) from whom the deity was adopted by Indradyumna, the king of Malava, who constructed the temple and installed the wooden idol of the deity there. The king Indradyumna is a mythical character and no historical account is available on him. There are also propositions of the origin of Jagannath cult from Buddhism,

Jainism and Hinduism, each of which goes with its own rational interpretations.

In the temple of Jagannath no caste rule of Hindu hierarchical system is implied in regard to the *Mahaprasada* and all the people irrespective of their caste are treated as equal while distributing *Mahaprasada*. Customarily *Mahaprasada* is to be eaten sitting on floor irrespective of one's status. This very feature, i.e., the absence of caste system is one of the strong points in favour of the Buddhist origin of the deity. Rejecting it the argument from Hindu point of view tells that eating of *Mahaprasada* by all castes from the same plate is a custom also found in the Hindu temples at Bhubaneswara and outside Odisha (*ibid*: 95). Likewise there are lots of arguments in favour of all the theories countering each other.

However, the Sabaras place a strong claim over the deity. Till date they have specific role in the daily *seba*, i.e., the ritual service to the deity. The Sabara *Sebakas* (*Sebaka*= the servitor to the deity) are commonly called as Daita. During certain important festivities like *Ratha Yatra*, the most famous car-festival of Lord Jagannath, *Snan Yatra*, the bathing ceremony of the Lord and *Anabasar,* a period of 15 days preceding to *Snan Yatra*, the Daitas have specific services (*seba)* to the deity. During *Anabasar* the deity remains under the control of Daitas and the temple remains closed for all others.

There is difference of opinions among the scholars regarding the dating of the Jagannath temple at Puri. However, according to Bengal District Gazetteers of Puri (1908; rep. 2007: 28) the present temple was built in the first half of the 12th century A.D. by Chodaganga Dev, the most powerful of the Eastern Ganga kings. Under the patronage of Ganga kings Jagannath became the tutelary deity of the royal family. Jagannath is worshipped in association with two other deities namely Balabhadra, the elder brother of Lord Krishna and Subhadra, their sister. After installation of the wooden images of Jagannath, Balabhadra and Subhadra in that temple the king declared himself as the *Sebaka* (servitor) of Lord Jagannath. It is stated in Odisha State Gazetteer (Vol. I,

1990, p. 9) that 'Under Chodogangadeva (12th century), Vaishnavism was firmly rooted in Odisha. Ramanuja came to Puri sometimes between 1122 and 1137 A.D., and gave a strong impetus to Vaishnavism. ... Ramanuja tried to bring about certain changes in the worship of Jagannath but there was strong opposition. Although Jagannath came to be regarded as an incarnation of Vishnu, a separate temple was constructed in the compound of the temple of Jagannath at Puri to install Lakshmi, the consort of Vishnu.'

The same Gazetteer (p. 11) also stated that 'Jagannath has been described as Vishnu in a copper plate grant of Narasimhadeva IV. In the same copper plate it is mentioned that Gangesvardeva had constructed the temple of Jagannath. Narasimhadeva flourished in the 14th century A.D.' According to recently discovered copper plates of the Ganga dynasty (internet source), the construction of the existing Jagannath temple was initiated by the ruler of Kalinga, Anantavarman Chodaganga Dev. The *Jagamohana* and the *Vimana* portions of the temple were built during his reign (1078 - 1148 CE). However it was only in the year 1174 CE that the Odishan ruler Ananga Bhima Deva rebuilt the temple to give a shape in which it stands today. It is said that the construction of the temple took 14 years to complete and was consecrated in 1198 CE. Like Ganga kings, the kings of succeeding Surya dynasty also made extensive endowments in land and jwelleries for the deities.

The temple continued to be under the Hindu rulers till the reign of Mukunda Deva who secured the throne in 1560 and was the last independent Hindu king of Odisha. In 1564-65 Mukunda Deva concluded a treaty with the Mughal Emperor Akbar to counterpoise the attacks of Afghans of Bengal but the measure did not help him for long. In 1567 Ibrahim, the Golkonda king conquered the north of the country and next year the Afghan Nawab of Bengal attacked Mukunda Deva and defeated him. The Afgan General Illahabad Kalapahar ravaged Odisha and the temple of Puri (Bengal District Gazetteer of Puri, pp. 30-32). After the death of the Afghan king in 1573 the Mughals established their rule over Odisha but soon the land was relinquished to the Afghans. In 1590, Mughal Emperor Akbar appointed his Hindu general Raja Mansingh, Governor of Bihar, who defeated the Afghans and annexed Odisha into the Mughal dominion in 1591 (ibid, pp. 32-33). In 1568-69, following the death of Mukunda Deva, Ramai Rautra, who was a son of a minister of the Bhoi dynasty seized the western part of Puri district and established his capital at Khurda. He brought the sacred relics of Jagannath and consecrated them in the temple with much pomp and solemnity. Subsequently, in 1590, the Afghans ceded Puri and its temple to Man Singh. For some time Man Singh appears to have kept the Jagannath temple in his own hands, but eventually he placed the shrine in the charge of Khurda Raja, who maintained the worship with great splendour and founded several colonies of Brahmans in villages. Henceforward the history of the Khurda Rajas is closely connected with that of the temple (ibid, 46). Odisha remained under the Mughals till 1751 A.D. when Marathas overpowered Ali Vardi Khan, the Nawab of Bengal. In 1756 the Marathas obtained the governorship of Odisha and from that day till 1803 Odisha remained a Maratha province (ibid, pp. 39-40). The British annexed Odisha into British Empire in 1803.

Temple Administration Through Ages

The administration of the temple was regulated by the Rulers, whosoever in power, until the advent of the British into the scenario. The Ganga Rulers and the successive Suryavanshi and Bhoi kings contributed a lot towards the development of the temple administration. Mughals imposed 'Pilgrim Tax' on the visitors of the Jagannath temple. Pilgrim Tax was continued by the Marathas also. They also took interest in the development and improvement of the temple. Later, on annexing Odisha into their territory in 1803, British took over the temple administration but the association with a Hindu temple was not supported by the British Parliament. As a result one superintendent was appointed by the government to run the administration. Later on the king was vested with the power of superintendent. It is the British who streamlined the administration in a systematic way. The pilgrim tax was abolished by the British under Act X of 1840.

After Independence of the country the Government of Odisha assumed full control over the temple. With a view to keep the administration in order 'The Puri Shri Jagannath Temple (Administration) Act' was passed by the government in 1952 where a provision has been made to prepare the record of rights and duties of *Sebayats* (*Sebakas*) and such other persons who were associated with the system of worship and management of the temple. Subsequently a special Act known as Shri Jagannath Temple Act 1955 was enacted to reorganise the scheme of management of the temple and its properties. The Act brought into force with effect from 27.12. 1960. In terms of the provision of this Act the management, administration and governance of the temple was vested on a committee known as Shri Jagannath Temple Managing Committee which constituted of the King (Dajapati Maharaj) of Puri as Chairman, the Collector and District Magistrate of Puri as Vice Chairman, Administrator, Shri Jagannath Temple, who would be an ex-officio member, the Commissioner of Endowment, who again would be an ex-officio member, one nominated member who would be entitled to sit at Muktimandapa, four members from *Sebakas*, one nominated member representing the Mathas and alike institutions associated with *sebapuja* or *nitis* of the temple, two nominated members by the state government other than last three categories. In the present administrative structure, the committee, called Puri Jagannath Temple Committee, constituted under section 5 of Sri Jagannath Temple Act (amended in 2004) and comprising of 18 members having representation both from the *Sevakas* and from the government functionaries. Temple Committee members are selected and appointed by the government of Odisha. The king (Gajapati Maharaj) hereditarily holds the position of Chairman of the committee. The Collector of Puri District, the Additional Secretary, Law Department, the Superintendent of Police, the Superintending Archaeologist, Archaeological Survey of India, Bhubaneswar Circle, the Commissioner of Endowments, appointed under the Odisha Hindu Religious Act 1951, all are the Ex-Officio member of the committee. The office of the working Chairman is not below the rank of Additional Chief Secretary. The Chief Administrator, appointed under sub-section (1) of section 19, is the ex-officio member from the rank of R.D.C. (Revenue Commissioner) and functions as Secretary. He works through three Administrators who are not members of the temple committee. They are Administrator-Niti, Administrator-Development and Administrator-Security. The first is empowered to look after *niti,* i.e., the ceremonies which make up the daily ritual.

The rules regulating these ceremonies are contained in the sacred book namely Niladri Mohodaya. Presently the worship is performed in accordance with the procedure laid down here. The book contains ninety one chapters giving detailed description about the various festivals of Lord Jagannath apart from the rules regarding daily worship of the lord. Another such sacred book containing temple rituals is Bamdev Samhita. After taking over the charge by the Government of Odisha the Records-of-Right has been prepared under the Puri Sri Jagannath Temple Administration Act (Odisha Act XIV of 1952) and that is followed thereafter. The word *niti* in Oriya literally means a rule but in the temple usage it refers to rituals and religious rights. The *nitis* are elaborate and complex and involves *seba* (service) and *Sebakas* (servitors to the god). The Administrator-Niti is assisted by two Assistant Administrators who are the staff of temple administration. Administrator-Development looks after the revenue and property matters of the temple besides various construction works for the temple.

The temple has huge immovable properties like cultivable land, quarries, waterbodies, etc., which form its major sources of earnings. Such properties came as gift from the kings and aristocrats from different corners of the country in different times. The construction works are done through two Deputy Administrators and one Assistant Administrator who are government employees. The Deputy Administrators gets assistance from temple administrative stuff. The temple also has various sources of earnings besides donation in cash and kind including *Dhwaja* (flags of ritual importance) and ornaments from the *Bhaktas*. Besides, it receives yearly grant for festivals and establishment from the Government apart from special grant on specific occasion. The *Sebakas* receive honourarium against their services from the temple fund only. The committee has representation of five *Sebakas* who were nominated by the Government of Odisha. The Chief Administrator picks up some names from *Chhattisanijoga* and sends to the Government. After being scrutinised through Law department regarding the behaviour, social reputation and police records of the proposed candidates, five members from them are selected and being formally approved by the Chief Minister of Odisha they are appointed as members of the Committee through a notification by the Law Department. They are supposed to offer necessary guidance for *sebapuja* according to the Records-of-Rights 1952. Besides, one member is to be nominated by the Government of Odisha from those who are entitled to sit at the *Muktimandapa* (the hall so named), the seat of the Sasana Brahmins. These groups of Brahmanas are not of local origin; they were actually brought by the kings from northern India. Separate villages were developed for them and they were given free hand to control social affairs of their respective villages. Such villages were designated as *Sasana* villages and the Brahmans were referred to as *sasana* Brahmans. They have no direct bearings to *seba* or services to the God but they are relied upon by the kings for cultivation of *Sastra* (books of traditional Hindu laws and scriptures). Every member of the committee excepting the Chairman and the Ex-Officio members shall hold the office for a period of three years from the date of notification and are eligible for re-nomination.

The committee is responsible for smooth functioning of temple activities including *sebapuja* and *niti* in accordance to the Records of Right, facilities to the pilgrims, maintenance of temple properties, both movable and immovable ones, maintenance of law and order and hygienic condition within the walled compound of the temple, payment of emoluments to its salaried staff, spending of donation according to the wish of the donor and so on. The daily activities of the temple is highly disciplined and organised. All the Mathas come under the administration of the Commissioner of Endowment.

Sebapuja and *Sebaka*: The Tradition

The Jagannath temple is having an elaborate system of daily worship to the Gods. This daily worship involves several specific ritual services, i.e., *sebapuja* that start from early morning and continued till late evening around 11.00 pm. The Ganga kings introduced *sebapuja* to the deities and it is continuing till date. The people assigned with the duties of *sebapuja,* (i.e., the servitors to the God) are called *Sebaka.* Each and every kind of service to the God is a *seba* and for each *seba* there is a *Sebaka. Sebakas* are not necessarily from Brahman caste only. For different kinds of *seba*, *Sebakas* were appointed from different castes. The Brahman *Sebakas* are popularly called *Pandā*. Initially there were nine *Sebakas*. They were *Caru Hota*, *Patra Hota*, *Brahma*, *Acharya*, *Pratihari*, *Puspalaka*, *Daita*, the washerman and the barber. The services of *Sebakas* were later extended to 36 categories, known as *Chhattisa Niyoga*/ *Nijoga* (*chhattisa*=36, *nijoga*/ *niyoga*= a class or an association). *Chhattisa Nijoga* involves a number of *nijogas*. They are *Pratiharinijoga*, *Suar* or *Mahasuarnijoga*, *Bhitar Sebakanijoga*, *Pujapandanijoga* and many others. They were responsible for smooth functioning of *sebapuja*. The heads of the *nijoga* were called *Nayaka*. Above all there was *Patjoshi* who ensured proper functioning of the temple. *Chhattisa Nijoga* is headed by *Chhattisa Nijoga* Mahapatra who enjoys authority over the temple functionaries. He supervises the execution of all orders by the temple authorities. He belongs to the *Puspalak* category of *Sebaka*. The *seba* categories might have further extended over time. The temple Record of Rights, 1952, recorded 119 categories (appendix 1) of *Sebakas* but presently all of them are not functional.

Pratiharinijoga is responsible to maintain law and order

inside the temple premise. They enforce discipline among the visitors and devotees within the walled compound of the temple. Besides they are also assigned with specific duties of messenger between certain temple functionaries. Until they formally invite, the kitchen mates cannot bring *Bhoga* (food for the Gods) to the main temple.

Bhitarchha Mahapatra is a single member *seba* category. He looks after the smooth functioning of the *sebapuja*, opening of the temple gates in the morning and checks the seals on the doors. *Suar* or *Mahasuarnijoga* is responsible for preparation of *bhoga* and looks after the maintenance of *rasashala* (the temple kitchen). *Suar* is a derivation of the word *Supakar* meaning the cook. They are the largest *Nijoga* of the temple.

Pujapandanijoga is the association or assemblage of priest-*Sebakas*. They compulsorily belong to Brahman caste. There is no one other than Puja Pandā can offer priestly services to the deities.

The *Sebakas* enjoy hereditary right for *sebapuja*. There are innumerable numbers of ritual service or *seba* around the deities and each *Sebaka* was traditionally assigned with a particular ritual service to the deity. The responsibility of each *Sebaka* is fixed and can never be overlapping. Nobody encroaches into other's functional jurisdiction. On death of a *Sebaka* his right to *seba* goes to his male heir. But to ensure the proper service to the Gods he is to undergo a test before a committee headed by *Chhattisa Nijoga* Mahapatra where he is to prove his perfection in knowledge about his duty. After being satisfied with the test the *Chhattisa Nijoga* Mahapatra declares him fit for *seba* and assigns him with his right to *seba* through an initiation ceremony called *Saribandha*. Through this ceremony *a Sebaka* gets confirmation of his inclusion in the *Sebaka* group.

By virtue of his hereditary rights, the king of Puri, honourably referred to as Gajapati Maharaj, enjoys the status of *Adya Sebaka* (the first servitor) to Lord Jagannath. He has specific ritual services to perform on specific occasions. The *seba* or services of the king towards the deities succeeds in male line and rule of primogeniture is maintained, i.e., the eldest son of the king succeeds as the *Adya Sebaka*. The younger son(s) of the king would be Thakur Raja or the Thakraj.

Each *Sebaka* is entitled to receive a share (*khei*) of the *prasada* (the food offered to the Gods and get sanctified through rituals is called *prasada*). The *prasada* of Jagannath temple is called *mahaprasada* (*maha*=great). The king enjoys a major *khei*. Other *Sebakas* also receive *khei* according to their entitlement. Keeping in view the huge growth of population in each lineage of *Sebaka* over time, a system of *pali* (a turn of service) had been introduced which is a social control over the hereditary right of *seba*. *Pali* fixes the schedule of service for each *Sebaka*. It is a system which ensures each family under a *Sebaka*-lineage to get a turn for offering *seba* to the Gods and thereby to earn its *khei* of *prasada* by fixing the day or days of service (*seba*) for each family. Each of the *Sebaka* family offers its services to the deities on the fixed day or days as hereditary right. *Pali* is controlled by the respective *Nijoga*. The *Sebakas* having *pali* are called *Palia*. *Pali* is a well organised and disciplined system. The name of each *Palia* is enrolled in the temple office and they are called for their respective services accordingly. One can transfer his *Pali* to other *Palia* on occurrence of death or any sudden emergency in the family. The right to *seba* inherits in the male line, i.e., from father to son(s) and it is strictly a men's domain.

Each *Sebaka* was assigned to a particular kind of *seba* by the king and that became their hereditary right. Till date the system is continuing unchanged. Each and every *seba* involve traditional knowledge. The *sebas* are well defined and so are the duties of *Sebakas*. Nobody encroaches into other's functional jurisdiction.

In appeasing Lord Jagannath, Pandās or *Sebakas* play the role of a mediator between the God and the people (*Bhakta*). People can make their offerings to the deity through Pandās only and the Pandās perform *Puja* (worship) for the devotees (*Bhakta*). There are specific categories of Pandās for specific services (*seba*) to the deity like Puja- Pandā performs the *seba* of worship; Pratihari-Pandā performs their specific *seba* besides maintaining *warja* and so on. Like wise for each and every *seba* to the deity there is one category of *Sebakas* and no interference is allowed in each other's right. "*Seba* is a duty to the *Sebaka* and their very existence is meant for that. It is our primary duty and we are to leave all other jobs to perform *seba* to the Lord. We feel ourselves privileged that we offer *seba* to the God. I am now working in a shop as salesman as my father and elder brother are offering *seba* to the God. But when my turn will come I will leave the job and join as *Sebaka* because that is my first and foremost duty..." says a young member of a *Sebaka* family.

During the menstruation period of the female members in one's family, the concerned *Sebaka* does not perform *seba* in the temple for seven days. The practice is locally known as *maruchuya*.

Warja, *Jajmani* System and State-office

In the temple of Lord Jagannath, the Pratiharis were traditionally assigned to the duty of conducting pilgrims and to maintain the records of the visitors by the kings. They were also sent as religious messengers to all corners of India to propagate the glory of Lord Jagannath. They became popular as Pandā (the priest) among the devotees. Because they used to attend the pilgrims, popularly referred to as *jatri*, they were often referred to as *Jatri*-Pandā also. In olden days of Mughal and Maratha Ruling they used to collect the Pilgrim Tax for the government. For different states in India there were respective Pandās who used to conduct the piigrimage and each Pandā was restricted to his allotted zone only. The area-division among these Pratihāri Pandās was very systematic and nobody entered into other's zone. In course of their repeated visit to the limited places and to the limited people they became familiar to those people and whenever any pilgrimage is organised in their respective jurisdiction these Pratihāri Pandās were contacted by the devotees (*Bhakta/ Jatri*). This relationship between a Pandā family and a *Bhakta* family is maintained through generations and this continued interaction over a long period produced a socio-religious bond between the two, what precisely we can call *Jajmani* system. This bond brings a *Bhakta* to a particular priest often and thereby develops a reciprocal dependency on each other as service receiver and service provider.

The *jajmani* relations between the Pandā and the *Bhakta* assured their interactions over generations. Such relationship was carried forward generation after generation from father to son(s). Therefore the records about a particular family lineage kept on updated over generations and thereby could generate genealogical information. Thus, there developed the tradition of *warja*, the genealogical records. The working jurisdiction (area of *jajmani*) for each Pratihāri-Pandā is well defined since the days of kingly ruling and is maintained till date. In later days a few other categories of *Sebaka* were also included in maintaining the records of the *Jatris*. One instance of such case is recorded in the present study where a Khuntia *Sebaka* is maintaining *warjā* for the state of Uttar Pradesh (the case has been detailed later under Chandan Hajuri Estate).

Like the right to *seba*, the territory assigned to a Pratihāri-Pandā is also considered as the usufruct right for his descendents. Thus, the *jajmani* relations could be maintained over generations. It is the Jātri-Pandā who maintains the genealogical records of the pilgrims. It may be stated here that maintaining *warja* and attending pilgrims is a *seba* to the God for them.

The *jajmani* relations elevated the status of a Pratihāri-Pandā to that of a *guru* (the spiritual teacher) for the *jajmans*. Nowadays they call themselves as *Tirtha-guru* (tirtha=pilgrimage centre). In due course these *Gurus* or Pandās established their independent offices, popularly referred to as State-office, which institutionalised the tradition of *warja* in an organised way. Each state-office has definite working jurisdiction. A state-office may have one or more state under its control, sometimes it controls one or two districts only depending on the cleavage among the heirs. The State-offices are usually named after the founder Pandā like Bada Harihar Sing Guru estate, Bhagirath Gangadhar Mahapatra Estate; some are popularly referred after the name of the *jajmani* area like Simla state office, Keonjhar office, Nepal state office, Panjabi Math, South India state office and so on.

Genealogical Records and Traditional Knowledge

It has already been pointed out that the practice of maintaining genealogical records (*warja*) is a part of the total system of the temple oriented activities (*sebā*) involving specialised knowledge. The knowledge is transmitted from one generation to another in vertical order in male line.

The information regarding the devotee is recorded in a very systematic and elaborate fashion mentioning the state, district, taluka, thana (Police Station), village and family, one belongs to. Records are maintained at two levels: *dashkhati* and *warja*. *Dashkhathi* is the entry register. The word *Dashkhati* is derived from *dashkhat* meaning signature. It is so named as the devotee or the visitor is to sign in this register. As soon as a *Bhakta* approaches the state office he has to enter his name in *dashkhati*, the sign-*bahi* (*bahi*=book) mentioning the name of the state, district, taluka, thana, village he belongs to, his father's and grand father's name and confirming his presence he has to put his signature in the specified column. Then the *dashkhati* book is sent to office for locating the previous records in *warja*. From *warja* the *Bhakta* is informed about his ancestors and updates the record with the current information. *Warja* is maintained and updated time to time on the basis of the information provided by the *bhakta* in the *dashkhat bahi*. *Dashkhati* is necessarily filled in by the *Bhaktas* themselves.

In *warja* the entry is made in an order of the state name first, followed by the district, thana (Police Station) and village name. The second step is the entry of the name of the *Bhakta's* ancestor followed by the name of his/her father. Accordingly the state-office traces out the earlier reference of the devotee's family and updates the record with the later arrivals in the family. Records are maintained in alphabetical order. The following chart shows the methods of maintaining the genealogical records:

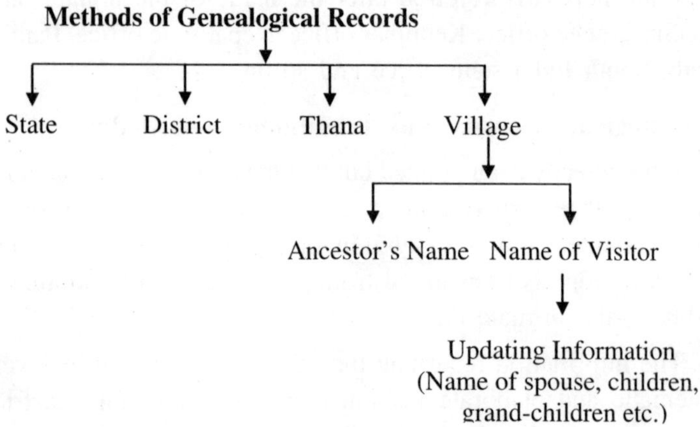

Fig. 2.

In ancient times both *warja* and *dashkhati* were written on palm-leaves, locally called *talapatra* (*tala*=palm tree, *patra*=leaf); in later ages machine made paper came into use. But in both the media the method of keeping the records is same, i.e., same procedure is maintained over time and thus there is continuity.

For writing on *talapatra*, a *lohar kalam* (*lohār*=of iron, *kalam*=pen) is used which is nothing but a small stick of solid iron. Palm-leaves *(talapatra) were* used to tie up in bunch with sacred thread (*paita*) only.

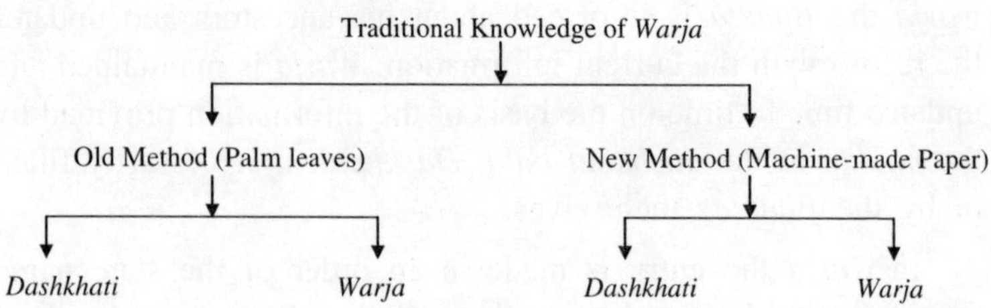

Fig. 3.

The Pandās often received *sananda*, the certificate of recognition, from the kings of different Princely States, mostly on copper plates (*Tamrapatra*; *Tamra*=copper, *Patra*=leaf or plate) through which the king declares the Pandā as the family priest for the purpose of making pilgrimage to Jagannath *Dham* by him and his family. These are maintained by the Pandās as family property. They continue to receive pilgrims from those areas till date.

Development and Functioning of State-offices

State-offices are the outcome of *jajmani* relations between the Pratihari-Pandā and the devotees, the *jatris*. With a holy intention of pilgrimage to Lord Jagannath the *Bhaktas* come from different corners of the country and approach their respective family Pandā for religious services and other hospitality. Because of the increasing pressure of *jajmans* day by day it became essential at one point of time to establish a kind of set-up that would provide better services to the pilgrims and maintained the *jajmani* relations in a better way. As the different *Jatri-pandas* were meant for particular areas or states of India (like Uttar Pradesh, Bihar, West Bengal, Rajasthan, Madhya Pradesh and so on) such establishments became popularly known as state-offices. It has already been mentioned that state-offices are the institutionalised *jajmani* system of which the ultimate product is the *warja*. Each state office maintains *warja* for the pilgrims of the respective state(s) under their control. State-offices are owned by the respective Pratihari-Pandā or Jatri-Pandā who hold the position of *Tirtha-guru*. The proprietorship of these state-offices is inherited strictly in the male line, i.e., from father to son(s). In case there is no son the inheritace of *Sebaka*-hood of a man will go to his brother, on his death the next male heir. Each state-office maintains a library of *warja* and provides service to their *jajmans*. The state-offices also take care of the local hospitality of the *jajmans*. Many have constructed their own guest-house (*jatrinivas*) and assure shelter and *Prasada* to their *jajmans*.

State-offices are headed by the *Tirtha-guru*, who is

compulsorily a direct male descendant of the founder Pandā. He is the highest authority of the state office. Each state-office has a definite working zone and each is restricted to its respective zone only. This particular area or the controlling zone is the hereditary right for the particular family of Pandā.

Tirtha-guru earns great respect from the *Bhaktas* who depend on the *guru* not just for their local hospitality but for the religious emancipation of soul as well. The *gurus* are regarded as the moving Jagannath by the *Bhaktas* and they ceremonially wash their feet and take their leftover food as *prasāda*.

The state-offices are devoted to the welfare of the *Bhaktas/ Jatri*, their *jajmans*. The office works according to the area of *jajmani* relations of the *Pandās*. Each state office has its own administrative body. *Tirtha-guru* is the hereditary chief and the proprietor of the state-office. Other office bearers are appointed by the *Tirtha-guru*. They are the salaried staff and follow the orders of the chief. The number of staff varies from one state-office to another depending on the requirement and the designations also vary. It is the responsibility of the *Tirtha-guru* to make the *jajmans* satisfied with their religious aspirations.

State-offices are independent in their activities. But their services to their *jajmans* are no other than a part of the temple activities (*seba*). It has already been discussed that the working jurisdiction of a *Pratihari-Pandā* passes on to the next generation as a hereditary right in the male line, i.e., from father to son(s) and all the sons have right to *seba*. Sometimes the state office is maintained jointly by the heirs; sometimes they maintain the *seba* independently. In later cases the working territory is mutually distributed by the sons among themselves and develops independent state-offices. The size of the *warja* library and the administrative body depends on the size of the working jurisdiction directly; more the working area more the size of the library and the number of functionaries. For small state-offices *Tirtha-guru* runs his office with limited number of *Chharidar* while an elaborate and well organised administration with the posts *Dewanji*, *Gomasta*,

Bato Gomasta is found in big state-office like Bada Harihar Sing Guru Estate. In another big state-office, popularly called Nepal Bhavan, there is one *Gomasta* and a good number of *Chharidar*.

CASE STUDIES OF SOME STATE-OFFICES

The basic style of working is same for all the state-offices with some individual variations in institutional structure especially in the administrative body. Some of them are discussed below.

Bada Harihar Singh Guru Estate

This state office has a large jurisdiction over a number of states namely Bihar, Jharkhand, Uttar Pradesh, Uttaranchal, Madhya Pradesh, Chhattishgarh, West Bengal, Nepal, Rajasthan and Hariyana. Presently the state office is headed by Sri Satyanarayan Guru who holds the honourable position of *Tirthaguru*. He is a male line descendent of the founder *Jatri-*Pandā. The *jajmans* regard him as a living god, a *guru*. The office was established by his forefather Sri Harihar Singh Guru who was popularly known as Bada Harihar Singh and therefore the office was so named. "Harihar Singh earned high reputation in those days and his *jajmans* included the *Rajas* (kings) of a few princely states in Uttar Pradesh and Rajasthan" informs Sri Satyanarayan. The office is having *sananda* (certificate of recognition) from the Rajas on copper plate (*tāmra-patra*) and also on paper; some of them are still preserved in the office. *Sanandas* exhibited to the present researchers are written in Devanagari script, some are inscribed on metallic plates and some are written on paper. The *sanandas* affirm the acceptance of Sri Harihar Singh Guru as *guru* for not only for the then family members of the king but assure the same for the future generation also. Thereby a *jajmani* relation had been established. The estate has old palm-leave *warja* and paper *warja* in their custody but those are decaying in natural course. Some of the earlier documents are written in old Karana language which is obsolete now and cannot be retrieved into existing *warja bahi*.

This state-office is having a *warja* library. It has its own working machinery. The office bearers include *Dewanji*, *Gomasta* and *Chharidar* who are assigned with different kinds of job. They are the employees appointed by *Tirthaguru*, the chief of the state-office. *Dewanji* looks after the *warja* library, maintains the records in good condition and keeps on updating the records as soon as added information are available. The duty of the *Gomasta* is to receive the *Bhaktas*, to look after their local hospitality and to escort them to the *Puja Pandā* for offering puja. *Chharidars*, also called *Bato-Gomasta* are the messengers of *Tirtha-guru*. They go to the distant areas, keep contact with the *jajmans*, conduct pilgrimage for the state-office, collect the pilgrims from the railway stations or bus terminus, bring them to the state-office and take them to the temple for *darshana* (the holy sight of Lord Jagannath). For the state-office they are the grass-root level workers. They are the linkmen between the state office and the *jatri* or the devotees. They go to the villages and to the people on behalf of the *Tirtha-guru*.

The office has an elaborate regulatory mechanism. As soon a devotee reports the state-office he is to register his name in the *daskhati bahi* with the following information:

1. the place of his origin with name of the district, state, village, thana, i.e., Police Station, post office,
2. name of his father, grand-father and great grand-father,
3. name of his children, their marital status, their children, if any, and so on.

After furnishing all informations the devotee is to sign his full name. Then this *daskhati* register would go to *Dewanji* who immediately locates the *warja* on the basis of information provided in *daskhati* and narrates the recorded information about his forefathers to the devotee. At the same time the earlier record is updated with the recent informations. Both *daskhati* and *warja* are arranged in alphabetical order for easy handling.

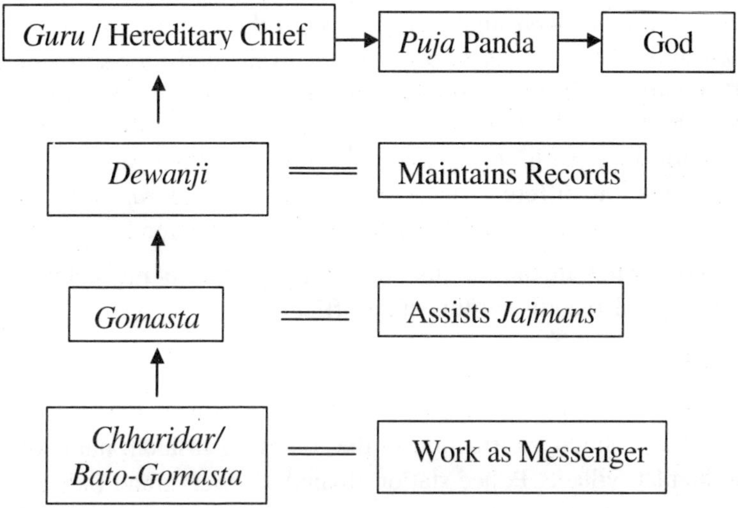

Fig. 4.

The *Bhaktas* offer their worship through *Puja Pandā* who are the priest *Sevakas* of the temple. The estate arranges food, lodging and transportation for the *Bhaktas*. Food is arranged from the temple kitchen only, i.e., the *Bhoga-mandapa bhoga* which is cooked for public and saleable to the devotees, to various *Matha*, state-offices and to the people associated with the temple.

Besides, Sri Satyanarayan Guru has also specific *seba* to the deity as *Sebaka*.

Bhagirath Gangadhar Mahapatra Estate

This state office is presently headed by Sri Rabinarayan Pandā and Sri Suryanarayan Pandā, who inherited the office from their father. As the name implies the founder *Sebaka* was Bhagirath Gangadhar Mahapatra who was assigned with such duties by the king. The present proprietors of the office are the direct descendent of him. Their jurisdiction is Keonjhar and Kalahandi districts of Odisha, Jamsedpur, Paschim (West) Singbhum and districts of Medinipur and 24 Parganas of West Bengal. It is stated by the proprietors that this particular Pandā lineage is called Raj Pandā because one of its descendent became Raja or the king. According to them the oldest *warja* traceable in this office is about 100 years old. Besides keeping *warja* they enjoy the right to *Gorabaru sebā*, *Pratihari sebā* and *Harap sebā* to the deities. *Gorabaru sebā* allows the *Sebaka* to serve water to the deity for some or other purpose. In this particular case the servitors supply water from the holy well of the temple on bathing ceremony of the God, the lord Jagannath. *Pratihari sebā* involves their service as messenger on different occasion of *sebapuja*. *Harap seba* is the serving of *pan* (betel leaf) to the deity after food.

Followings are the various steps or the methods of maintaining genealogical records by this state office:

Daskhati

In *daskhati* or the signing register the devotees themselves enter the required information in the following fashion: name of the hamlet, village, Police station (thana), district, grand father's name, present devotee's name, his wife's name if married and then signature. All these information then will be transferred to the *warja* by the office bearer under the supervision of the Pandā.

Suchipatra

For *warja* a content register or *suchipatra* is maintained according to the *Pargana*, Post Office, village, all alphabetically arranged, and then page numbers which help them to locate the particular *warja* book instantly.

Pargana ⟶ P.O. ⟶ Village ⟶ Page Number

Warja

For each Zilla or district there is separate *warja* book. Under the district village names are arranged alphabetically. Whenever any old *warja* book turns spoiled the data have immediately been copied down to a new book in same order of entry and replace the old one.

Office Bearers

The owner Pandā of this State office is called *Tirtha-guru* (literally the teacher for the pilgrimage; *tirtha*=pilgrimage, *guru*=teacher) who is the direct descendent of the founder

Sebaka. Here both Sri Suryanarayan Pandā and Sri Rabinarayan Pandā are *Tirtha-gurus*. Under them there are *Chharidar*, also called *Gomasta* who receives the *jajmans*, takes them around the temple for *darshana*, gets them *prasāda*, and takes them to *Pujā* Pandā whosoever on duty (*pālā*) for offering *pujā*. They also maintain the *daskhati* and *warja* books.

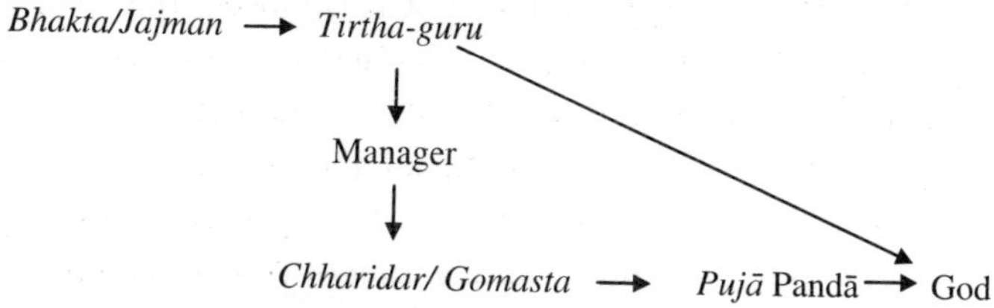

Fig. 5.

(*Pujā* Pandā is not a member of any state office. He is the priest to the deities at the temple. In the temple of lord Jagannath only the Pujā Pandā is allowed to perform the priestly job).

There are fifteen *Chharidar* working in this state office. *Chharidar* are employees only but some of them are attached to the state office over generations. Manager is also an employee. He looks after the smooth functioning of the office and takes care of the hospitality of the *jajmans* who come on pilgrimage.

Tirtha-guru is respectable to the *jajmans* and through him the *jajmans* (the devotees) aim to earn salvation. In turn by providing religious service to the *jajmans, Tirtha-guru* offers his *sebā* to the God and thereby earns virtues.

Like many others this state office also runs a *Dharmsāla* (the religious inn) where the *jajmans* are accommodated during their stay at Puri. The state office also provides food and other hospitalities to the *jajmans*, get them *prasāda*, take them to the *Pujā* Pandā for offering their worship to the God.

Nepal Bhavan

The proprietor of this state office is Sri Madhab Mahapatra, who succeeded as Tirthaguru from his father. *Pratihari sebā* and *Khuntiā sebā* are his other assignments. He is often referred to as Nepali Pandā as the jurisdiction of his *jajmani* relation includes Nepal along with part of Assam and two districts of North Bengal namely Jalpaiguri and Darjeeling. He informed that the king of Nepal awarded his forefather with the title of 'Lalmoria' and thus, this state office is popularly known as Lalmoria Estate and they also prefix the title with their name. Their forefather, from whom the tradition continued, was Bhimsen Mahapatra who was assigned with the Pratihari *sebā* and was allotted the areas of Nepal, Assam and Northern Bengal to popularise the name of lord Jagannath. "The king of Nepal though is not a *Sebayat* (servitors to lord Jagannath) but enjoys special honour in the Jagannath temple. It is none but the king of Nepal, who presented the *salgram* (holy black stone) for the *ratna-singhasan* or *ratna-bedi* (the elevated seat for lord Jagannath and his associates in the sanctum sanctorum of the temple) of the Gods" as stated by Sri Madhab Mahapatra.

The records of the pilgrims are maintained in the same fashion as of other state offices.

Daskhati

The first step is *Daskhati*, the signature book where the entry is made by the devotees themselves with their signature to authenticate the information. The information entered in *Daskhati* are name of the devotee, father's name, grand father's name, name of the district, village he hailed from, spouse's name, children if any, grand children if any. All these informations are then transferred to *warja* book by the office bearer.

Warja

Warja is maintained according to the district and village name, arranged in alphabetical order. Old and spoiled *warja* are replaced immediately and the data have been restored with special care. A spacious *warja* library is maintained in this state office. *Warja* books are arranged separately according to the State and the district. Under the district, village names come in alphabetical order.

State ⟶ District ⟶ Village

Example:

Nepal	District A	Village a, b, c,...
	District B	Village a, b, c,...
	District C	Village a, b, c,...and so on..

In *warja* the book number and page number of the particular *daskhati* is noted for reference; say book no. x, page no. y means the corresponding *daskhati* register bears the said number and said page number. It helps to match two registers as and when required. There were old palm leaf *warja* in the custody of this state office but those are now in a shape beyond preservation. Presently they maintain and preserve the *warja* written on paper only.

Suchipatra

A content register or *Suchipatra* is maintained to locate the *warja* book. In this content register the district names are written in alphabetical order. Under each district the village names are catalogued, again in alphabetical order. For each state of India and for the country of Nepal there is separate content register. For instance along with the name of a particular district and village the suchipatra also shows *warja* book number and page number.

Office Bearers

Tirthaguru earns high respect from the *jajmans*. He runs his office through *Chharidār* who are employees only but mostly have association with this state office through generations. The duties of the *Chharidār* are to receive the *jajmans*, to take them around the temple, to maintain the *daskhati* and *warja* books and to help the devotees in all respect to complete their pilgrimage. This state office has no separate office bearer as Manager. The *Tirthaguru* himself carries out the managerial tasks. This state office maintains its own *dharamsālā* (accommodation for the pilgrims) where the *jajmans* are given accommodation during their pilgrimage at Puri. During the present field work the *dharamsālā* was almost full with devotees from Nepal and from the district of Darjeeling and Jalpaiguri. The *Tirthaguru* personally takes care of their well being, takes them to the temple for worship, and makes arrangement for their food and *Mahaprasada* from the temple. He believes that the *jajmans* are the responsibility of the *Tirthaguru* and he is to make their pilgrimage successful.

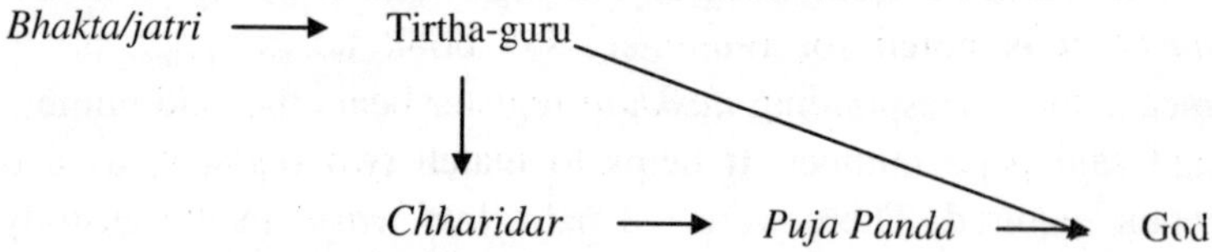

Fig. 6.

Besides, he has *Pratihari sebā* and *Gorabaru sebā* to the temple and Sri Madhab Mahapatra gets his *Pāli* on 12th and on 29th day in a month for *Pratihari sebā* and once in every 68 days for *Gorabaru sebā*. Whenever any article is carried into the temple it is the duty of the Pratihari to take an account of the article first and only after satisfaction he allows to take the article inside the temple.

Sri Madhab Mahapatra feels it is now time to utilise the technological advancement of the day. As he says, "I wish to computerise the whole *warja* information that is in my custody. For that I am to talk to some computer expert. It would help me for better preservation of the *warja* documents."

South India State Office

They call it *warja*. This office is popularly called Telegu Pandā state office. It covers the entire south India (Andhra Pradesh, Tamil Nadu, Kerala, and Karnataka) and Goa (Konkon). Its jurisdiction also includes Jodhpur area of Rajasthan. The founder Pandā of this state office was Ramachandra Pratihari, also called Ramachandra Bhagaban Pandā. Presently the office is run by

Rajat Pratihari, a direct descent of the founder Pandā. He succeeded the office as he is the eldest among two brothers of his generation. His younger brother, Ipsit Kumar Pratihari, is also associated with the state office and looks after the official activities. The Telegu people call them Pontulu Pandā. In Telegu language Pontulu denotes a teacher or a Brahman; traditionally a Brahman used to be addressed or referred to as Pontulu. It is claimed that this state office is as old as of the temple. This office is also known as Atharobhai state office, as informed by Sri Rajat Pratihari. Similar to other state offices this office also follows the same methods of daskhati and *warija* for preserving the genealogical records.

Daskhati

As soon as a devotee reaches the state office he is to enter the following information in *Daskhati* register: the name of the district, tahsil, Thana (Police station), and village he is hailed from. "Suppose a person presently resides at Salt Lake in Kolkata but actually hails from Medinipur then he is to write Medinipur as district name followed by the names of tahsil, and so on. If there is absolutely nobody of the lineage lives in Medinipur then only he can add the address of Salt Lake as *prastut thikana* (ready address)" explains Sri Rajat Kumar Pratihari. For a male *jajman* father's and grand father's names are essential while for a female devotee names of father-in-law and grand father-in-law are to be mentioned. Besides, he or she is to provide the added information like name of spouse, sons, if adult, their business/ profession, their spouses' name, grand children, if there is any, and lastly the devotee is to sign with date to authenticate the information provided by him or her. With these added information immediately the *warija* records are updated. There are about 200 *daskhati* registers in this office.

Warija

Warija, according to them is the duplicate book where the information provided by the devotees is copied down by the Pandā for their own use. Entries in *warija* are maintained according to the date of entry in the *daskhati* register. *Warija* books are arranged in the following order: first comes district, then taluka followed by villages, all arranged in alphabetical order.

Warija
- District A
  - Taluka A — Village A, B, C etcetera
  - Taluka B — Village A, B, C etcetera
  - Taluka C — Village A, B, C etcetera
  - And so on
- District B
  - Taluka A1 — Village A, B, C etcetera
  - Taluka B1 and so on
- District C
  - Taluka A2 — Village A, B, C etcetera
  - Taluka B2 — Village A, B, C etcetera
  - And so on.

Fig. 7.

"In olden days the *daskhati* and *warija* were written on palm leaves but all those got spoiled long back. Now we have paper *warija* only" says Sri Pratihari. In *warija* books against any entry the book number and page number of *daskhati* register are mentioned as reference so that the two register can be tallied at any time.

Office Bearers

Tirtha-guru is the highest honour, the post occupied by Sri Rajat Pratihari, the present owner of this state office. Next to him in the order is his brother, who helps *Tirtha-guru* in running the office. All other office bearers are employees though many of them are associated through generations. Among the employees there are *Gomasta*, three in number, who take care of the maintenance of *daskhati* and *warija* documents. In case any old *daskhati* or *warija* book gets spoiled they are copied down in ditto into new books immediately and thereby data have been restored. *Gomasta* are assigned to such job. Besides there are *Chharidar*, altogether ten in number, who attend the *jatri* (the devotees) and conduct the pilgrimage. They also visit the villages, organise the devotees for pilgrimage on behalf of the *Tirtha-guru* and bring them to the state office. Precisely they are field level workers who collect information about the devotees, keep contact with them and look after their wellbeing when they are on pilgrimage at Puri.

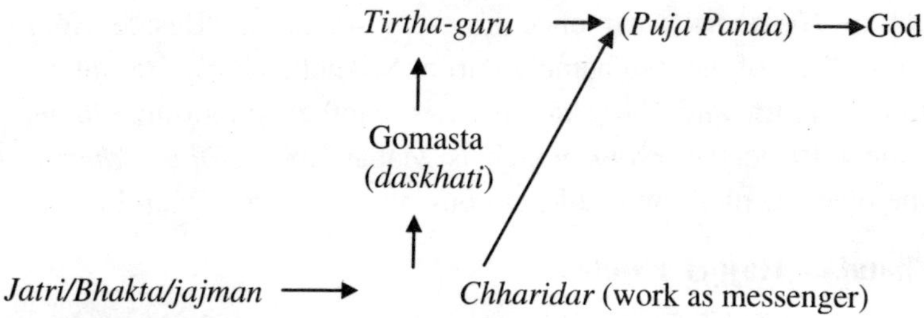

Fig. 8.

Nowadays the *Chharidars* need not to visit the distant villages every time due to cell phone facility. They contact the pilgrims over phone and arrange the programmes accordingly. 'Earlier sometimes it happened that the *Bhaktas* had to take money on loan from the Pandā and whenever the *Chharidar* visited their places they used to return the money through him' observed one of the *Chharidar*. "Many of the *Gomasta* who were associated with this or other such offices some 20 years back have now taken up the job of *Jatri* Pandā and running their business independently of their own" informs Sri Pratihari.

Besides running this state office Sri Rajat Pratihari enjoys the right of three kinds of *seba* namely Pratihari *seba*, Gorabaru *seba* and Hadapnayaka *seba*. Hadapnayaka is one who serves *pan* (betel leaf) to the deities after food. Besides, on the festive occasions Hadapnayaka is to supply pan to the deities in bulk. During Chandan Yatra, a famous festival observed in the month of *Baisakha* (April-May), one hundred pieces of *pan* is to be offered. *Pan* is presented in *khili* (rolled in typical fashion) and instead of lime paste (which is usually used with betel), *chandan* (sandal paste) is smeared on the leaf. On Gorabaru *seba* he supplies water for the deities. During the *snanyatra*, the bathing ceremony of lord Jagannath he brings water from *Sona kuya*, the holy well, for the God, offer water during *Sona Besha* (a type of dress) of lord Jagannath during Paus *Purnima* (the full moon day in the month of *Pausa*, i.e., December-January). On the observance of the day when the temple was consecrated, he offers *ghee* (clarified butter) with which the lord is given a bath. He gets a turn of *Hadapnayaka seba* once in every 40 days and that of *Gorabaru seba* once in every 48 days. "Besides four major *dham* of the lord namely Puri or Srikhetra (Puri), Badrinath, Rameswaram and Dwarka, there is another important *dham*, namely Brindaban *dham* which is Mahaprabhu's *bihar khetra*" (the place of pleasure or of amorous play) adds Sri Rajat Kumar.

Chandan Hajuri Estate

They call it *warija*. This state office is presently headed by Hajuri Bhimsen Khuntia, a male line descendent of Sri Chandan Hajuri, the founder Pandā. It is claimed that 'Hajuri' is a title which their forefathers were awarded with by the King. Therefore they prefix the title with their names though people often suffix the title while referring or addressing them. The working jurisdiction of this state office covers the whole of Uttar Pradesh. "This office was established in the year 1857 by Sri Chandan Hajuri. His direct descendant was Sri Nilkanta Hajuri, who was a Jury in British Court of Law" informs Sri Bhimsen Hajuri. Their *seba* to the God is that of Khuntia. Duty of the Khuntia is to monitor the activities which have direct concern to the presiding deity, lord Jagannath; they are likely the bodyguard of the lord. The Khuntia on duty is to bring flower and holy basil for the deity which they handover to *Sringari Sebaka* who is assigned with the specific duty to adorn the lord. It is the duty of the Khuntia to wake up the lord in the morning and he is the last person to leave lord's bed room at night after completion of the scheduled rituals of *sayan* (divine sleep) of the deity. In a day three people from Khuntia *Sebaka* would be on duty to lord Jagannath. One would guard the lord and other two would keep vigilance on the people around Jagannath so that nobody touches him. They get their *pali* on fixed dates and it is the responsibility of the temple administration to inform the *Palias* about their *pali*. Normally they get *pali* for three days in every 34 days. Hajuri Ramnarayan

Khuntia, a brother of Bhimsen informs that they get their *pali* on 3rd, 5th, 8th and 25th days of a span of every 34 days. They are registered *sevaka* and had been succeeded the *seba* through *saribandha* ceremony.

Daskhati

On reaching to the state office a *jatri* registers his name in *Daskhati* with the following details: names of the district, tahsil, thana (Police station), mauja, village he belongs to, name of his father, grandfather and great grandfather (*tin pirhi*, i.e., three generation), his own *gotra*, name of his wife, names of his children, their spouses, if married, and children, if any. He is to authenticate the entry by putting his signature at the end. For a female devotee the names of her husband, father-in-law and grandfather-in-law are to be furnished. She is also to provide information about her children, if any, their marital status and their children and so on. According to Sri Bhimsen the earliest record preserved in their custody dates 150 years back.

Warija

In their words '*warija* can be called *nakal* (copy) *bahi*' as the information is copied down from the original *bahi* (book) of *daskhati*. *Daskhati* is considered as original *bahi* as the entries in this register are made by the devotees themselves and are authenticated with their signature. *Warija* is maintained for the use of the state office only. In *warija* the information on a particular family or lineage, picked up from the *daskhati*, are arranged in a systematic manner so that all the information regarding a family can be found out immediately. As soon as added information is available in *daskhati* on a particular family it is incorporated immediately in the *warija*, thereby updating it constantly. In *warija*, informations are recorded in the following fashion:

District ⟶ village ⟶ names of 3 generation ⟶ devotee's name ⟶ *gotra*

This state office has records of 150 years old.

Office Bearers

Bhimsen Hajuri, the owner and the head of this state office

is regarded as *Tirthaguru.* His brothers, Sri Krishna Chandra, Sri Ramnarayan and Sri Rabinarayan help him in running the office. They also receive high regards from the devotees. Other posts are Manager, *Gomasta* and *Chharidar*, all salaried employees. There are altogether five numbers of *Gomasta*, three numbers of *Chharidar* and one Manager, all work under *Tirthaguru. Chharidars* write the *warija* books, *Gomasta*s look after the *jatris*; they collect the *jatris*, the *jajmans* from the stations or bus stand whenever they arrive on pilgrimage, arrange their stay at Puri, take them around the temple and to the Puja Pandā for offering their *puja* to the God and look after for their comforts during their stay at Puri.

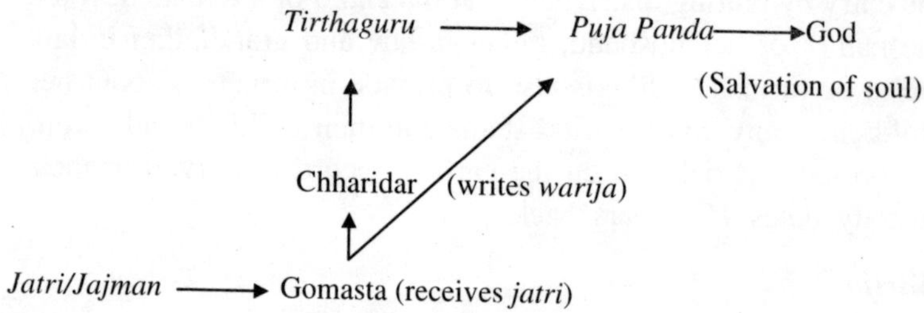

Fig. 9.

Satjug Estate

Popularly known as Shimla Bhaban, this office was established at least about four generations back. The present proprietor is Nabakishor Sinhari, who being eldest among his brothers succeeded this office as *Tirthagurus* from his father Late Ramdayal Sinhari. Ramdayal was the eldest son of late Ganesh Ram Sinhari who succeeded the office from his father Chintamoni Sinhari. The eldest son succeeds as *Tirthaguru* while all the sons succeed as *sevapuja* equally. The working jurisdiction of this state office includes the states of Himachal Pradesh, Jharkhand, Odisha and West Bengal (now Paschimbanga).

In the words of Nabakishor Sinhari "our forefather, in those days, visited the court of Shimla king and propagated the glory of lord Jagannath there. The king was highly impressed with his words and behaviour and sent his people to him for pilgrimage to the lord. Since then people from Shimla comes to our family for pilgrimage. The family expanded in natural process over time and presently it is a joint family of about 100 members." This state-office receives *jajman* from the Shimla and Solan districts of Himachal Pradesh, East Singhbhum district of Jharkhand, Kandhamal and Narayangarh (Dashapalla area) districts of Odisha and West Medinipur district (Lachipur and Gopalpur area) of west Bengal. Nowadays number of *jatri* from Shimla has been decreased.

Daskhati Khata

In *daskhati khata* the entries are made by the *jajman* or the *jatri* only. First, a *jatri* is to write his full address with the names of the village, post office, tehsil, district and the state he or she belongs to. Nowadays the *jajmans* are required to provide their mobile phone numbers and postal Pin codes of the area. Next entry is the *jajman*'s name along with spouse's name, followed by his father's name, grand father's name, number of brothers, where they live, the name of children including brother's children and at the end of the entries the *jajman* has to sign. Signature authenticates the information provided by the *jajman*.

Warija

In *warija* the informations are copied down from *daskhati* with the mention of date on which the jajman visited the state office and who accompanied him. *Warija* registers are maintained district wise, and are arrayed in their office library in alphabetical order for an easy access. Overall supervision is done by Sri Nabakishor Sinhari but for running the day to day business there are six employees in different official capacity. Of them two are designated as Managers, four are *Chharidars*. Besides, there is one *jharudar* (sweeper). Duty of *Chharidars* includes:

1. to organise pilgrimage and to receive the *jajmans* from the railway station or bus stand wherever the *jajmans* arrive at Puri,

2. to make arrangement of their stay at Puri,
3. to make necessary arrangement so that the pilgrims gets *prasada*, especially the *annabhog*,
4. to take the *jajmans* to the temple for *darshana*,
5. to take the *jajmans* around the temple complex for *darshana* of all other deities,
6. to look after the comfort of the *jajmans*.

The state office has its own *bhaban* (guest-house) for the pilgrims and the *jajmans* are preferably accommodated there. Free accommodations are provided in the guest-house. In case a *jajman* wishes to stay in a hotel, the Chharidar makes arrangement accordingly. Traditionally a *Chharidar* was to visit the *jajmani* areas of *Tirthaguru* on a regular interval to bring pilgrims to the state office but nowadays they do not visit the places in a routine manner and depend mainly on telephone to keep contact with the *jajmans.* Sometimes the *jajmans* intimate the state office prior to their arrival, sometimes they do not. The state office never charges any money against its services from a *jajman*, but conventionally *jajmans* pay donation to the state office on satisfactory completion of their pilgrimage. The Pandā, i.e., the *Tirthaguru* receives *pranami* from the *jajmans*. *Chharidars* are often remunerated by the *jajmans* as a token of reward for their service.

The traditional *seba* of this family is that of sinhari or *sringari* (adoring of the deities). *Pali* comes once in every 14 days. *Sringaris* have their own *nijoga*, i.e., pushpalok *nijoga*, entry to which as *Sebaka* demands an examination to be passed by the successor. The examination is to be organised by the *nijoga*. The successful *Sebaka* joins his duty with due permission from Gajapati Maharaj, Temple Administration and Patjoshi Mahapatra. Nowadays examination is becoming compulsory for the successors of any category of *Sebaka*.

Preservation and Conservation

For palm leaf inscription only young leaves were used. Before taking into use the leaves were left in the open air for six to seven days for drying up and then cut into pieces. After recording the documents, the palm leaf pieces were set one upon another between two hard boards and tied with sacred thread. Periodically the records were kept exposed to sunlight and camphor (*coppur*) and *gonuk* were applied as paste control preservatives. *Gonuk* is a kind of locally available plant. Now-a-days they use naphthalene and other modern pesticides for preservation.

The old *tala-patra warja* are preserved with proper care but inspite of their attention many of the *talopatra warja* are getting damaged in its normal course. The data from palm leaf *warja* could not be transcribed as the script used in olden days became obsolete in due course.

Nowadays both *warja* and *dashkhati* are maintained on paper only. They also take care of the old and spoiled records. Old spoiled registers, both *dashkhati* and *warja*, are replaced by the new one and the data from spoiled one are transferred in ditto to the new registers. For such work people with good handwriting are employed temporarily.

Observation

The whole system of *warja* stands on the religious beliefs and myths and maintained through the *jajmani* relations between the devotees, i.e., the *Bhaktas* and the Pratihari Pandās or the *Tirthagurus*. The *jajmani* relation has its foothold on the dependency of the devotees on the priests for achieving *moksha,* the ultimate spiritual salvation. The priests act as mediators between the devotees and the God, sometimes a priest is even elevated to the status of the living representative of the God. They are regarded as the living Jagannath by the devotees and are worshipped with great devotion. The *Tirthagurus* in their turn look after the welfare of the *Bhaktas* and it is their submission that through the service to the devotees they are actually serving to the God. So the relationship is important for both and it forms the very basis of the continuity of the *warja* tradition.

State offices are the later development of the *jajmani* system. It institutionalised the tradition and contributes effectively towards the maintenance of the practice. Maintaining *warja* and service to the devotees is considered as a *seba* to the deity and it is popularly called *jatri seba or Jatri Pandā seba*. *Jatri seba* is a part of Pratihari *seba*. Besides, the whole system acts as the economic resource to a huge population, not only for the *Sebakas* but also for the people who are associated with the tradition in some way or other. The employment in and association with the state-offices further extends the horizon of traditional knowledge and expertise beyond the group of Pandā and it is learnt that many of the *Chharidars* and *Gomasta* who once served the *Tirthagurus* of one or the other state-offices are now running their own business of *Jatriseba*, the service to the devotees.

It is informed by the *Tirthagurus* that this genealogical record of *warja* is so famous and recognised practice that it is taken as a valid document in cases of property inheritance by the court of Law and they often supply Xerox copies of the document. According to one key resource personnel these are not used in court as document in very recent times. Whatsoever the recent development is, the *warja* records have been accepted as valid information of the family or lineage or *bansabali* across the societies. It has tremendous potentiality to generate knowledge about the Indian society and its pattern of pilgrimage.

Inspite of changing power structure over historical period and political turmoil of the State of Odisha through centuries the tradition of the temple services is continuing through the daily *seba*, ritual functions and exercising rights over *seba* by the *Sebakas*, carrying with them the traditional knowledge system. Interestingly there is absolutely no change in the practices of *seba* and the duties of the *Sebakas* since the days of the kingly ruling and so is the tradition of *warja*. Continuity is maintained strictly.

Keeping in view the increasing population pressure in the field of *seba*, nowadays there is a tendency among the young generation to shift to other occupations like white-collar jobs, business, teaching and so on. But because of the hereditary right to *seba* they prefer to be employed within the city. To them *seba* is their prime duty of life. They are attached to their traditional role not only through their religious beliefs but also morally and emotionally which form an integral part of their life, their cultural tradition in which they live.

There is much dissatisfaction among the *Sebakas* as they feel that due to the impact of tourism, their age-old *jajmani* system is advancing towards a threat. They look for the economic support from the Government as well as from the temple administration.

Acknowledgement

We express our sincere gratitude to Prof K.K. Misra, Director, Anthropological Survey of India for his constant encouragement for anthropological researches. We are deeply indebted to the Temple committee of the Jagannath temple, Puri for their cooperation in every respect. Sri Sudip Chatterjee of temple administration deserves special mention for his untiring cooperation and guidance. His indepth knowledge about the temple activities, rituals and norms gave us an insight to the subject. Inspite of his busy schedule he attended our endless quiries, introduced us to the right persons for information. We owe him so much. Sri Laxmidhar Puja Pandā, being an insider, enlightened us with his vast knowledge and insight. He always attended us with smiling face even when he was facing several family problems. Sri Satyanarayan Guru of Bada Harihar Singh Guru Estate, inspite of his busy schedule attended us every time and enlightened us with his thorough knowledge, provided us an insight about the philosophical importance of the temple and extended his cooperation in every respect. We are thankful to all the people of his estate. We express our sincere gratitude to all the *Sebakas* of the Puri temple, whose cooperation and knowledge made this study successful.

References

Kamal K. Misra (2005) Indegenous Knowledge, Natural Resource Management and Development: The Konda Reddy Experience, Bhopal and New Delhi: IGRMS, Pratibha Prakashan.

O'Malley, L.S.S. (1908) Bengal District Gazetteers of Puri, Reprint 2007, Logos Press, New Delhi.

Behuria, Nrusingha Charan (1990) Odisha State Gazetteer, Odisha State, Vol. I.

Appendices

I. Myths and Legends Around the Temple

The popular legend associated with the temple and the deity goes like this: Lord Jagannath was secretly worshipped as Neelmadhaba by a Sabara (a tribe of Odisha) king named Viswabasu. He installed the deity in a secret cave deep into the forest and nobody other than him knew the place. Having heard about the deity, Indradyumna, the king of Malwa, wanted to propitiate the deity. With this purpose he sent a Brahman priest, namely Vidyapati, to locate the deity. The Sabara king refused to disclose the secret to him. Vidyapati tried his best to locate the deity but failed. But at last he managed to marry princess Lalita, the daughter of the Sabara king and earned the trust of Viswabasu. On repeated request of the son-in-law the king took him blind-folded to the cave where Neelmadhaba was installed. Vidyapati carried some mustard seeds with him and on his way to the cave he dropped those seeds on the ground without the knowledge of the Sabara king. The seeds germinated in a few days and he was able to locate the cave later on. Immediately he informed the king Indradyumna and the king started his jouney for the deity. But when the king approached the cave the deity disappeared. Being disappointed with the situation Indradyumna determined not to return without seeing the deity and to observe fast until the deity appears before him. Then he heard an astral voice directed him to receive the fragrant tree on the seashore and make idols out of it. Accordingly the king collected the fragrant tree but the question arose who would make the idol. Then Narada, the divine saint suggested to get the work done by Viswakarma. The celestial architect made the images of lord Jagannath, Balabhadra and Subhadra and the idols were installed in the temple.

It was a condition from the part of Viswakarma that he would make the images in a close door room being isolated and nobody should enter into the room until his work would complete. But the queen could not resist herself from a glimpse of the images under construction and she entered into the room. But she saw none but the incomplete images of the deities fashioned from the waist upwards having only stumps of arm for the images of Jagannath and his brother Balabhadra while their sister Subhadra had not at all. The creator left for ever. The images remained so till date.

(II) *Sorosopochār* Worship (worship with all 16 kinds of offerings; *soroso*=sixteen, *upachār*=items of offering to the deity, i.e., worship in all details):

1. *Asana* (seat)
2. *Swagata* (welcome)
3. *Padya*, wash of the feet of the God with water
4. *Arghya*, offering flower and sandal paste
5. *Achamaniya*, offering water for rinsing the mouth
6. *Madhuparka*, offering honey ghee, milk and curds on silver or copper vessel
7. *Achamaniya*, offering water for rinsing the mouth
8. *Snan* (bathing)
9. *Bastra* (offering clothings)
10. *Abhoran* (offering ornaments)
11. *Gandha*, offering of perfumes and sandal paste
12. *Pushpa* (offering flower)
13. *Dhupa* (offering incense)
14. *Pradip* (offering earthen lamp)
15. *Naibedya* (offering food before the idol)
16. *Bandana* (invocation/adoration)

***Panchopochar* Worship** (worship with five items of offerings; *Pancho*=five, *upachar*=items of offering to the deity):

1. *Chandana* (sandal paste)
2. *Pushpa* (flower)
3. *Dhupa* (offering incense)

4. *Deepa* (offering earthen lamp)
5. *Bastra and alankar* (cloths and ornaments)

(III) Mathas

There are a number of Mathas (the Hindu monastries) developed centering the temple of lord Jagannath. In olden days of king's ruling the Mathas had definite duties to be performed towards the worship of the lord.

A list of the Mathas at Puri is given below:

Dated	*Name of the Matha*	*Type, Sect (Sampradaya)*
6th century	Virgu Ashram	Angilā
7th century	Angirā "	-do-
9th century	Govardhana	Advaita
- do-	Sankarananda	-do-
10th century	Mahiprakasha	Brahmachari
12th century	Ramanuja Kota	Viśistādvaita
-do-	Trimāli	-do-
-do-	Bada Santha	-do-
-do-	Emāra Math	-do-
-do-	Sāna Santha	Gāduā Mādhava
-do-	Gopāla Tirtha	Adwaita
-do-	Siva Tirtha	-do-
-do-	Bada Jhādu	Angilā
13th century	Daśāvtara Matha	-do-
14th century	Languli Matha	Daśanami
-do-	Bada Chatā Matha	Angilā, Rāmānanda
15th century	Chāuni Matha	Angilā
-do-	Rāghavadāsa Matha	-do-
16th century	Kavira Caurā	Santhamata
-do-	Bāuli Matha	-do-
-do-	Sidha Bakuja Matha	Acintya Vedā Veda
-do-	Rādhā Kānta	-do-

Dated	*Name of the Matha*	*Type, Sect (Sampradaya)*
16th century	Gangāmātā	-do-
-do-	Haridākhandi Matha	Rāmānandi
-do-	Srirām Das Matha	Viśistādvaita
-do-	Narasimhācāri "	-do-
-do-	Sāna Jhādu	Angilā, Viśistādwaita
-do-	Kunja Matha	Goudiya
-do-	Śiśu Matha	Utkaliya Vaisnava
-do-	Cakra Tirtha Matha	Angilā, Viśistādwaita
-do-	Ghumusar Matha	Rāmānandi
-do-	Dagarā Matha	Angilā
-do-	Labanikhiā Matha	-do-
-do-	Purāna Savā Matha	-do-
-do-	Gandharva Matha	Utkaliya Vaisnava
-do-	Achyutā Matha	Goudiya
-do-	Goswāmi Matha	-do-
-do-	Śāta Lahari Matha	Ati Badi
-do-	Śāta Asana Matha	-do-
-do-	Haridās Matha	Acintyavedā Veda
-do-	Totā Gopinātha	-do-
-do-	Dukhiśyām Bābā Matha	Abadhūta
-do-	Bada Oriyā Matha	Ati Badi Gādwā Mādhava

(IV) List of various classes of *Sebakas* and others employed for and connected with the *Seba-Puja* of the Temple and its Endowments (As per Record of Rights).

1.	Gajapati Maharaja	2.	Raja Guru
3.	Pattajoshi Mahapatra	4.	Bhitarachha
5.	Talichha	6.	Mudarasta
7.	Deul Purahita	8.	Puja Panda
9.	Bada Panda	10.	Puspalaka
11.	Mahajana	12.	Mudra

13.	Khuntia	14.	Bhandar Mekap
15.	Palia Mekap	16.	Akhanda Mekapa
17.	Changada Mekapa	18.	Khata Seja Mekap
19.	Pratihari	20.	Dayita
21.	Pati Mahapatra	22.	Patri Badu
23.	Gara Badu	24.	Suar Badu
25.	Khuri Nayak	26.	Mikha Pakhala
27.	Ghatuari	28.	Gochhikara
29.	Suna Goswami	30.	Muduli
31.	Alati Balita Sevak	32.	Puran Panda
33.	Dutta Mahapatra	34.	Lugadhua and Panikunda Sevak
35.	Ballava Jogania	36.	Biman Badu
37.	Anasara Sudha Suar	38.	Hadapa Nayak
39.	Bidia Jogania	40.	Khatuli Sevak
41.	Asthana Patirhari	42.	Kotha bhoga Jogania
43.	Pradhani	44.	Paika
45.	Lenka	46.	Suar Nijoga Nayak
47.	Suar Nijoga and Mahasuar	48.	Jagia Mahasuar
49.	Badu Suar, Thali, Tunaa and Amalu Suar	50.	Panti Badu
51.	Amalu Tola, Pura Kharadi	52.	Tola Badu
53.	Rosa Paika	54.	Bahara Deuli Suar
55.	Bahara Deuli Jogania	56.	Rosa Dho Pakhalia, Angarua, Gobara Pania and Rabadia
57.	Handi Jogania Tola Bati	58.	Biri Munda SaMatha
59.	Kotha bhoga Pania	60.	Paniki Patta
61.	Nikapa and Gandhana Nikapa	62.	Biri Buha
63.	Daudi Bala	64.	Chunara

65.	Sabata Nijoga	66.	Pani Apata
67.	Mandani	68.	Chaka Apasara
69.	Mulia Suansia	70.	Binakara
71.	Darpania	72.	Kotha Suansia
73.	Maha Bhoi	74.	Gita Gobinda
75.	Bhitara Gayeni	76.	Samprada Nijoga
77.	Dayana Mali	78.	Madeli
79.	Prasada Badu, Badu Mahapatra	80.	Tatua
81.	Pattara Bandha	82.	Baijayanti
83.	Chhatara Nijoga	84.	Kahalia
85.	Sankhua	86.	Parba Tatra Jogania
87.	Chitrakara	88.	Rupakara
89.	Bania	90.	Damara Bisoi
91.	Karatia	92.	Benta Bindha Paika
93.	Patara Bisoi	94.	Kala Bethia
95.	Daraji Seva	96.	Kumbhar Bisoi
97.	Ratha Bhoi	98.	Mala Chula
99.	Banua	100.	Chakra Dihuri
101.	Ojha Maharana	102.	Ghanta Seva
103.	Ghantua	104.	Ratha Dahuka
105.	Badhei	106.	Baidya
107.	Amunhia Chhatar	108.	Chhamu Dihuri
109.	Chapa Behera	110.	Chapa Dalei
111.	Mapa Saita Karana	112.	Tadhau Karana
113.	Deula Karana	114.	Baithi Karana
115.	Kotha Karana	116.	Charcha Karana
117.	Dayana Patra	118.	Chaula Bachha Karana
119.	Matha and individual Seva		

(V) According to the Temple Record of Rites, the followings are the main *Nijogas* and their *seba* (assigned services to the God).

1. *Mudirasta:* Mudirasta represents the king. A young Brahmana boy below 18 years is selected for the purpose, whom the king appoints as his representative. He performs the *seva* of the king's part in his absence.
2. *Chhatisha Nijoga Mahapatra:* He is the overall incharge of the temple. He approves the *Sāri Bāndhā* ceremony, an initiation rite compulsory for a *Sevaka* before getting into the right to *seva* to the deity. Chatisha *Nijoga* Mahapatra supervises over the activities of the *Sevak*as. He is responsible to execute the orders of temple authorities. He belongs to the Puspalak family.
3. *Puja Pandā:* They are the priest and their responsibility is to perform *Puja*.
4. *Bitarachha Mahapatra:* He is the head of the temple for daily rituals. He keeps supervision on opening the doors in the morning and checks the seals. He also looks after the cleanliness of the foods offered to the Gods. He may enter into the kitchen which is a protected place and nobody other than Supakars (the cooks), Taluchha Mahapatra, Puja Pandā and Bitarachha Mahapatra are allowed inside the kitchens.
5. *Taluchha Mahapatra*: He seals the temple doors at night and also checks the cleanliness of the kitchen.
6. *Pradhani:* At the time of bringing food, he goes to the kitchen to invite goddess Lakshmi and the Suārs to come with Bhog; he then leads them to the inner sanctuary of the temple, makes a continuous sound with two pieces of canes to alert the people to keep the path clear.
7. *Deulakarana:* Traditionally they were the temple accountants. Now they handle some money matters, especially the donation money and distribute *prasada* to the devotees.
8. *Tadukarana:* He assists Deulakarana in account matters. He keeps accounts of the Bhandar, the store, affixes temple seals and posts dates of all special rituals or *niti*.

9. *Dayita:* They claim to be of Sabara (a tribe of Odisha) origin, the descendants of tribal chief Bishwabasu, who, according to the popular myth, worshipped Jagannath as Neela Madhava in the forest and from whom the deity was adopted by the King Indradyumna. Except *puja* (offer worship) and cooking, they do all the *sevā* to Lord Jagannath for one month from *Snana Purnima* to Rath Yatra. They are one of the major *Nijogas* of the temple. They believe Jagannath to be their own kith and kin.
10. *Khuntia Nijoga:* They are the body guards of the deities.
11. *Puja Pandā Nijoga:* They are the priest *Sevaka*. This is one of the most difficult services of the temple, because the Pujā Pandā must be thoroughly conversant with the norms and methods of worship. Formerly the knowledge used to transmit from father to sons but now the *Nijoga* conducts a course. It takes one to two years to train the young properly and then only a young Pujā Pandā can join the temple.
12. *Mekapa Nijoga:* They are in-charge of store. They are of four categories, namely Bhandara Mekapa, Khata seja Mekapa, Cangada Mekapa and Akhanda Mekapa, each having specific service to perform.
13. *Bhandara Makapa:* They are in-charge of the Bhāndār (store) containing all the gold ornaments, jewellery, diamonds precious stones for the deities.
14. *Pratihari Nijoga:* They guard the temple and enforce discipline among the visitors. Nowadays there are policemen who help them in this task. During the time of offering *bhoga* to the Gods it is the duty of the Pratiharis to go to the kitchen and ask to bring *bhoga* to the main temple. From the olden days Pratiharis used to keep records of the visiting pilgrims.
15. *Gochikars:* They help the Pratiharis in their tasks and guard the kitchen doors.

16. *Ghanta Nijoga:* They play cymbals called *ghanta* during the time of offering *bhoga* and during *pahandi.*
17. *Singhari Nijoga:* They are members of the Puspalak community who adorn the deities with dresses and flowers.
18. *Godabadu Nijoga:* They bring water from the temple well for *pujā* and other purposes.
19. *Sudha Suār:* They keep all *puja* items in their proper containers, for example, *chandana* (sandal paste) in the *chandana* pot and flowers on the flower trays and so on.
20. *Mudali:* They count and verify the number of *puja* utensils once *puja* is over. All utensils are supplied by Mekapas.
21. *Hadapanayaka Nijoga:* They offer *pān* (betal leaf) to the lord after every meal.
22. *Pania Apat:* They bring water and wash the floor where *bhoga* will be placed before the deities for the offering.
23. *Bimanbadu Nijoga:* They carry palanquins (*bimana*) of Lord Jagannath during the festival of *Chandan Yātrā*, observed on the third day of bright fortnight in the month of *Baisakha* (April-May) and continue for 42 days. The festival is observed in two stages, one the Bahara Chandana, and the other is Bhitara Chandana, each observed for 21 days. The former one is celebrated in a water body called Narendra Puskarini commonly called Narendra Tank and the later one is observed inside the temple. On the occasion of Bahara Chandana Madanmohona, the moving idol of Lord Jagannath is escorted in procession to Narendra Tank where the idol is placed on a boat and taken round the tank with dancing and music.
24. *Suar:* They are the cook of the temple kitchen. They are known differently according to the types of *bhoga* they cook. They are the biggest *Nijoga* of the temple.

25. *Chunera Nijoga:* The name Chunara is derived from *chuna* or lime. In olden days they used to apply whitewash to the temple. Now this job is done by labourers from outside.

The present-day duties of this *Nijoga* are as follows:

(a) To wave the flags daily from the temple-peak. The flags are to be tied with the *chakra* (the wheel) on the top of the temple. Until the new flags are waved, no *bhoga* can be offered. For carrying the flags to the *chakra* which is more than 215 feet high from the ground, one must climb more than 300 uneven stone steps through the outer temple wall. Today only one family is associated with this *seva.*

(b) They are in charge of worshipping *Garuda stambha* (the pillar of *Garuda, stambha*=pillar) in front of the main altar. *Garuda* is the *bahana* (the carrier) of Lord Vishnu. On the top of the pillar Garuda is seated with folded hands. Devotees embrace the piller and offer *pranāma* (bow).

(c) The members of this Nijoga carry a big lamp, known as *mahādipa*, on each *ekādasi* (eleventh day after the full moon day) to the temple-peak and place there.

(d) During *Deepāvali* (the Festival of Lights) in the month of *Kārtika* (October-November) members of this *Nijoga* decorate the temple with lights. On *Deva Deepāvali,* the festival of Light meant for Gods (*Deva*) the temple crest is decorated with small *dipa* (earthen lamps) by them.

(e) They are in charge of decorating *Aruna Stambha*, the Sun pillar (*Aruna*=Sun, *stambha*=pillar) outside the main entrance through eastern gate called *Simha dwar*, i.e., the lion's gate (*Simha*=Lion, *dwar*=gate) of the temple. The pillar is of stone, 34 feet in height and erected on a platform. *Aruna* is seated on the top of the pillar. The pillar was said to be constructed in 18th century A.D. All the devotees who visit the temple compulsorily make a *pranām* (bow down) to this pillar.

(VI)

Local Calendar	*English Calendar*
Baishakha (Oriya new-year)	April – May
Jyastha	May– June
Ashara	June – July
Shrabana	July – August
Bhadra	August – September
Aswina	September– October
Kartika	October- November
Margashira	November – December
Pausha	December – January
Magha	January – February
Phalguna	February – March
Chaitra	March - April

(VII) Data have been collected from following categories of sevaks:

1. Bhandar Makap
2. Bhitarchha Mahapatra
3. Biman Badu
4. Chunera
5. Deul Karan
6. Doita Poti
7. Ghantua
8. Godabadu
9. Khuntia
10. Kotha bhoga Pania
11. Mudali
12. Pani Apat
13. Pradhani
14. Puja Pandā
15. Pratihari
16. Sinhari/Srigari
17. Suar/Supakar
18. Sudha Suar

The Jagannath Temple at Puri, Odisha.

The Crowd of Devotees at the Jagannath Temple, Puri, Odisha.

Crowd during Rathayatra Festival, Jagannath Temple, Puri, Odisha.

Raja Performing his seba to the God as Adya Sebaka, Jagannath Temple, Puri.

Crowd of Devotees during Rathayatra, Puri, Odisha.

***Mahaprasada* of Lord Jagannatha, Puri.**

The Jagannath Temple, Puri, Odisha.

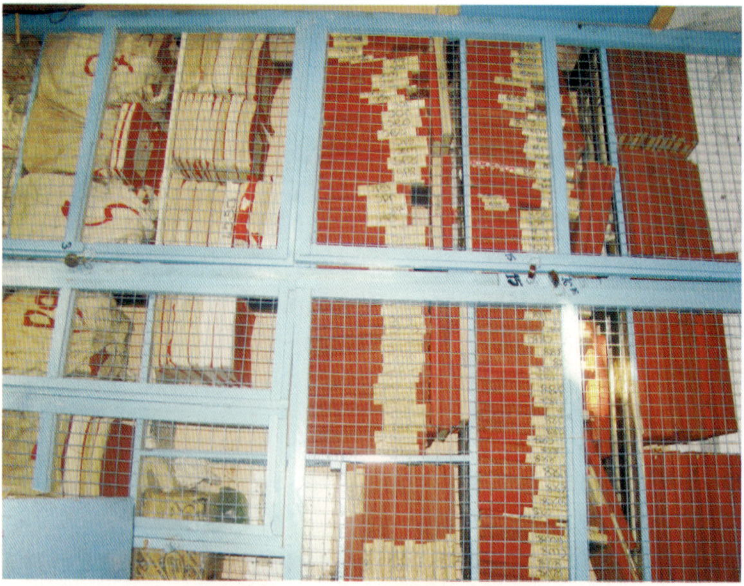

Warja Library of Bada Harihar Singh Guru Estate, Puri, Odisha.

Maintenance of *Warja* at Bada Harihar Singh Guru Estate, Puri, Odisha.

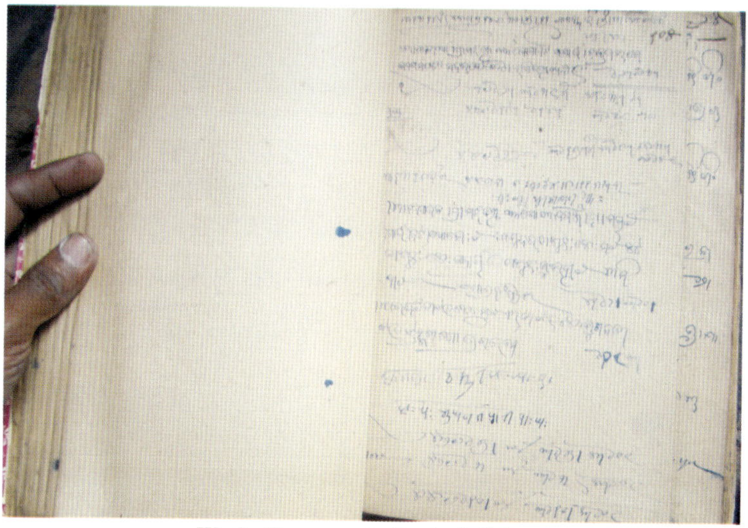

***Warja* Document, Puri, Odisha.**

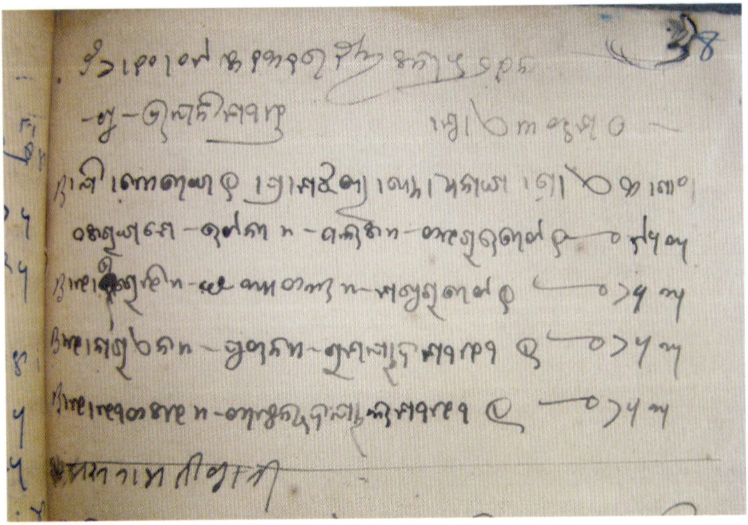

***Warja*, Puri, Odisha.**

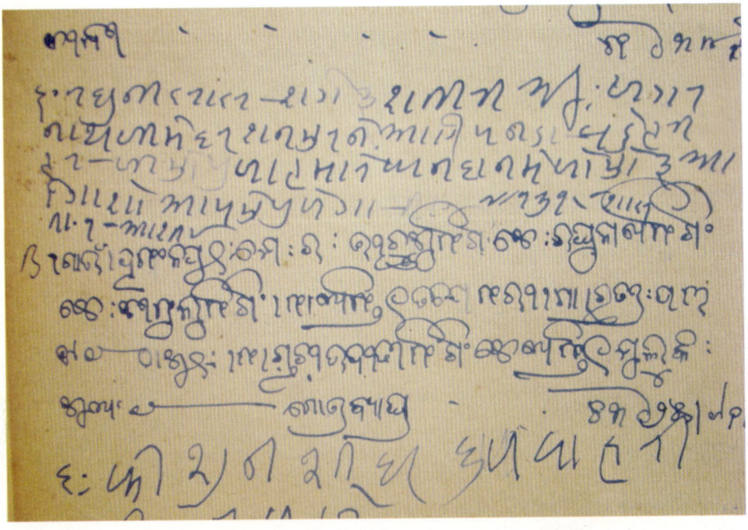

***Warja* Book, Entry Register, Puri, Odisha.**

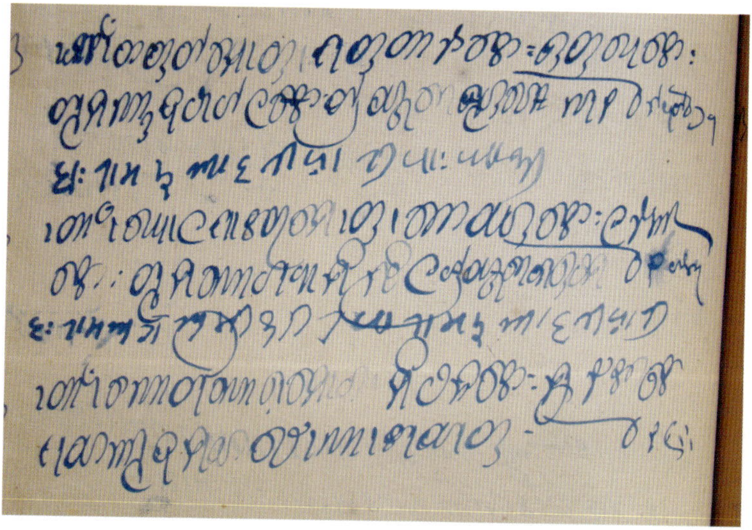

***Warja*, Puri, Odisha.**

***Sananda* on Copper Plate, Bada Harihar Singh Guru Estate, Puri, Odisha.**

Sananda at Bada Harihar Singh Guru Estate, Puri, Odisha.

2

The Tradition of *Banshabali* in the Sacred Centre of Haridwar: A Religious Significance of Hinduism

K.M. Sinha Roy

Introduction

The word Traditional knowledge has roofed a vast area of human social behaviour. It encompasses wisdom, knowledge and learning process of the communities. In many cases traditional knowledge has been orally passed over from person to person. Some forms of traditional knowledge are expressed through stories, legends, folklores, rituals, songs and even laws. Other forms of traditional knowledge are often expressed through different means like 'experience, trial and error and deliberate experiment' as has been discussed by Misra (2005:4). In the field of religion, traditional knowledge plays a crucial role in the areas of symbolic expression and its social values. In most of the sacred centers of India there is a tradition to maintain records of the devotees. The tradition is termed differently in different region. In the temple of Haridwar such records are called as *Banshabali*. Some primary information about the devotees is recorded in the *Banshabali* like the village, district and state from where the devotee is hailed from, his/her name and *gotra*. *Banshabali* helps one to trace his/her ancestral lineage and history of the particular family.

All over the globe, human being survives under the shade of religious umbrella. Religion involves a pattern of belief and a set of practices through which people establish a relationship with the supernatural power for spiritual and earthly wellbeing of self.

According to Encarta Encyclopedia (1997) Religion is "Sacred engagement with that which is believed to be a Spiritual Reality". The Webster dictionary defines religion as "Service and worship of God". Religions also have in common a set of values or conduct to be adhered to. This is an interesting point that though not all religions have the same set of precepts but in the vast majority the inner spirit ensures the physical and spiritual protection of the people.

The worship of God and the practice of meditation are assisted by external devices and symbols. Hinduism believes in images as concrete realisations of the Gods they symbolise. Idols are treated with great respect with an elaborate daily etiquette that includes rousing them from slumber, bathing them, and feeding them. A priest, the religious specialist has a culturally defined status. In Hindu religion, each sacred centre is having individual belief system

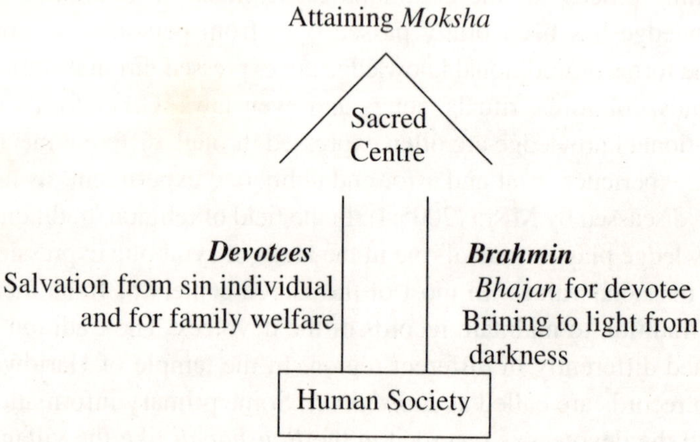

based on various legends and myths. The significance and value of a particular sacred centre is immense in human society. To overcome problems and for prosperity, people depend on religion in various ways. The religious mental make-up of the people, in fact, develops through the process of socialisation.

Religion dictates individuals about dos and don'ts for reaching the goal of spirituality. The sense of sin and virtue also comes into that realm. Human beings desire better lives, salvation from sin and to gain *moksha*, the ultimate salvation of soul. For fulfillment of their desire they need help of priests, here it is Brahmin who traditionally performs the priestly job. He is a link man between the sacred centre and the devotees. The devotees come to sacred centres for salvation from sin and welfare of individual or family members. In this way, the Brahmin, the devotees and the sacred centre enter into a relationship that continues from generation to generation. In this context Hardwar or Panchapuri has a great significance in the Hindu religion. The study tries to highlight religious significance of the place and role of Brahmin and of the record maintaining system in the field of religion.

Religious Significance of the Place

Hardwar is an ancient pilgrim centre of India. It is also known as gateway of the four *dham* (the house of God). Hardwar comprises of Jwalapur Mahavidyalaya, Gurukul Kangrilies on the right bank of the Ganga, at the southern base of the Siwalik range, through which, by a natural breach, river enters the plains, the width of which at its narrowest point is more than one km. On the left is the Chandi hill, on the top of which stands an ancient temple dedicated to goddess Durga. The derivation of the name Hardwar is debatable. The Shivaits claim the name Haradwara means Siva's gate (Hara=Lord Siva, dwara=gate). This is supported by the legend that the river Alaknanda (a branch of the River Ganga) was borne by Siva upon his head. The Vaishnavites, on the other hand, point triumphantly to the *Hari-ka- Charan* or *Har-ki-pauri* (Vishnu's footprint), as the indisputable evidence of the truth of their belief that the River Ganga has its rise in the nail of the great toe of Vishnu's left foot.

In the great epic of *Mahabharata*, Hardwar is mentioned as one of the places visited by Arjuna during his exile. It is said that the Pandāva brothers along with their wife Draupadi retired to the snowy range of the Himalayas passing through this town. According to the same text, Kapilasthana is still pointed out at Hardwar, so named after the sage Kapila who is said to have practiced religious austerities here.

Hiuen Tsang (629-645 A.D.) mentioned this town as Gangadwara, the name used by early Muslim chroniclers, Abu Rihan and Rashid-ud-din. About 1398 A.D., the town was plundered and devastated by Taimur, the central Asian invader. Abul Fazl, in the reign of Akbar (1556-1605 A.D.) referred to Hardwar where there was a mint for copper coin. Local tradition has it that Emperor Akbar used to be supplied with drinking water from Hardwar. In 1621, Emperor Jahangir visited Hardwar. In his reign (1605-1627 A.D.) the place was visited by Tom Coryat, a foreign traveller, who described it as the capital of Siva. In 1796, the town was visited by Hardwick, who called it a small place situated at the base of the hills. In 1803, after the British conquest of the upper Doab, it was included in the Saharanpur district.

Ablution in the holy River Ganga is the great religious rite practiced here by the pilgrims, their belief being that purgation from sin is thus obtained. According to the Hindu mythology king Bhagirath of Ikshvaku dynasty of Ayodhya, the ancestor of Lord Rama, was deputed to bring Ganga down to earth.

For the Hindus in India the River Ganga is regarded as holy; it is believed that a dip in the River Ganga washes off all sins. The dying person is given a sip of the holy water of Ganga with the belief that it will purify the departing soul. Before using water in daily prayers, it is supposed to be sanctified by a mantra containing the names of seven rivers of which the first is the Ganga (gange ca yamunecaiva etc). This river is considered to be so holy that Siva, God of the gods, holds her on His head. This holy river has evoked devotional fervour in the minds of the devotees through ages. Puranas, the ancient sacred scriptures, speak of seven streams of the Ganga: Bhagirathi, Caksuh, Hladini,

Nalini, Pavani Sindhu, Sita; of them Nalini, Haldini and Pavani flow towards east, Sita, Caksuh and Sindhu flow westward and Bhagirathi towards south.

The identification of the said rivers is done by the scholars of specialised fields. Of the seven streams, Bhagirathi and Sindhu are identified with the Ganga and the Indus respectively. The Caksuh presumed to be the Vaksu or VVaksu which is the Oxus or Amu Darya. The Sita may be the Tagdumbash branch of the Yarkand. The Hladini (or, Hradini) is tentatively identified with the upper Brahmaputra River. The Pavani is supposed, by some scholar to flow through Burma and identical with the Irawati. The identification of the Nalini remained difficult. It is said to have fallen into the sea in the saimi Mandala (Siam). This river is tentatively identified with the Salween or the Mekong.

The great object of attraction of Haridwar is the bathing ghat (bathing place on the bank of water body, here the river) called *Hari-ki Charan* or *Hari-ki pauri* (Vishnu's footprint). Other attractions for the tourists are the Birla tower and Man Singh-ki *Chhatri* (built during the reign of Emperor Akbar). Besides, there is Brahma–kund, a small temple in mid stream. This is perhaps the one that was noticed by Hiuen Tsang in 634 A.D. A bath in the kund is of great religious value as it is believed to be the spot where Lord Brahma, the creator, arranged the descent of the mother-goddess Ganga (River Ganga) to the earth. To the Hindus Ganga sanctifies both life and death. After sun set arti, i.e., worshipping of the deity with ritual lamps is performed. The most attractive part of it is the floated lighted *diyas* (traditional ritual lamps) down the river on boat shaped leaves. Priests of the temple line up on the *ghats* facing the river with lighted lamp in hand and *arti* song of Ganga is sung by the all the devotees and worshippers.

The empirical records show that the religious significance of the Hardwar is in the field of ancestral worship, *mundane*, *upanayan* (sacred thread wearing ceremony mandatory for the Brahmins), Ganga *snan* (bathing in Ganga) and Kumbha mela. The origin of Kumbha is legendary. The legend goes like this: there was a war between the *Devatas*, the Gods and *Asuras*, the demons over *Amrit Kalasha*, the pot with *amrita* (nectar, believed to be the source of immortality) which was emerged out of *Samudramanthan* (churning of the sea by Gods and demons). Both the parties wanted to catch hold of *amrita kalasha*. To prevent the Asuras, who were more powerful than Devatas, four of the Gods namely Brihaspati (the Jupiter), Surya (the Sun), Chandra (the Moon) and Shani (the Saturn) were entrusted for the safety of the *Amrit Kalasha*. The four *Devtas* ran away with the *Kalasha* to hide it from the *Asuras*. The four *Devatas* were running with *Amrita Kalasha*. The *Asuras* made a chase that lasted over day and night for 12 days round the earth and during this chase, Amrita dropped at four places namely Haridwar, Prayag, Ujjain and Nasik.

The Kumbha festival is most important for the Hindus; it is held in every 12 years as *Purna* Kumbha, i.e., full Kumbha and in every six years as *Ardha* Kumbha, i.e., half Kumbha. Millions of devotees, saints, priests and *yogis* from all corners of India take part in the celebrations. It is believed that bathing during Kumbh cures all sins and evils. The bathing commences in the month of *Chaitra* (March-April) when the sun enters the Zodical ring of *Mina* (Pisces) and concludes on the day when the luminary enters *Mesha* (Aries), agreeably to the solar computation of the Hindus, corresponding with 13th April every year. In every twelve years the planet Jupiter enters in the sign of Aquarius (kumbha), and the occasion is considered one of special sanctities, the fair being called the kumbha *mela*.

With all these religious occasions Haridwar stands as an important sacred centre for the Hindus and attract huge numbers of devotees from all corners of the country.

Genealogical Record (*Banshabali*)

As Haridwar is regarded as an ancient Hindu sacred centre, the local priest also addresses it as a Pancha puri. The essence of Haridwar is that devotees come to Pancha puri for spiritual satisfaction. The devotees come from different parts of the country as well as from abroad. In Hindu religious norm only the priest can offer worship to the deities and a priest is compulsorily from the Brahmin caste, the highest order in traditional social hierarchy. Therefore for every religious observances priest's service is compulsory and in this way an interdependent relationship is gradually built up between the priest and the devotees. Such relationship is called *Jajmani.* The *Jajmani* system gradually extends from one generation to another at individual or at family level. In the *Jajmani* system the devotees offer guru dhakhina (honourarium to the priest) in the form of cash, land and other materials and sometimes in the form of animal also. In return the priest helps the devotee getting salvation from all kind of sin and guides to attain *Moksha* (the ultimate salvation of soul). The priest maintains a record of the devotees in their own way. To keep the records properly, the priest applies some technique or method to trace out the earlier records easily. The practice of such system obviously involves traditional knowledge in the context of sacred centres of India.

In Hardwar, the *bansabali* records are maintained by two groups of priests namely *Tirtha Purohit* and Maha Brahmans, the former maintains the records for higher caste people, while the later maintains for scheduled castes. Both groups maintain records applying knowledge in the same way. The other Brahmin groups are not involved in such records maintaining system. The *Tirtha Purohits* usually sit at Kusha ghat on the bank of Ganga. Maha Brahmans also sit at Kusha ghat near the *Har-ki-pauri.* The place restricted for *Sradha* (death rituls), *Upanayan* (sacred thread wearing ceremony, observed by the Brahmins), *Mundan* (head shaving ceremony) and Ancestral worship. It is believed that the *Tirtha purohits* are immigrant to the area and came from Bengal during the reign of king Parikshyit. The legend says that Janmajoy, the son of Parikshyit, died of snake bite. In revenge the king arranged a *Yagnya* (the sacrificial fire) to kill the snakes. But local Brahmins refused to do the worship for him. Then the king brought the Brahmins from God (Gour) Bengal to perform the *Yagnya* and after completion of worship the Brahmins settled at Hardwar and adjacent areas.

The priests maintain the records for their respective *Jajmans.* The devotees come to their respective priest for worship. Accordingly, the priest records the preliminary information about the devotee, the name of the village, district the devotee is hailed from, caste identity, name of devotee, his *gotra* followed by his brother's name, father's name and grand father's name – all are written on the *Chopta* khata. *Chopta* is a register, which is also called entry book. Afterwards the priest transfers the information to another record book, the final one, which is known as *Bahi khata*.

Genealogical Record Maintaining System

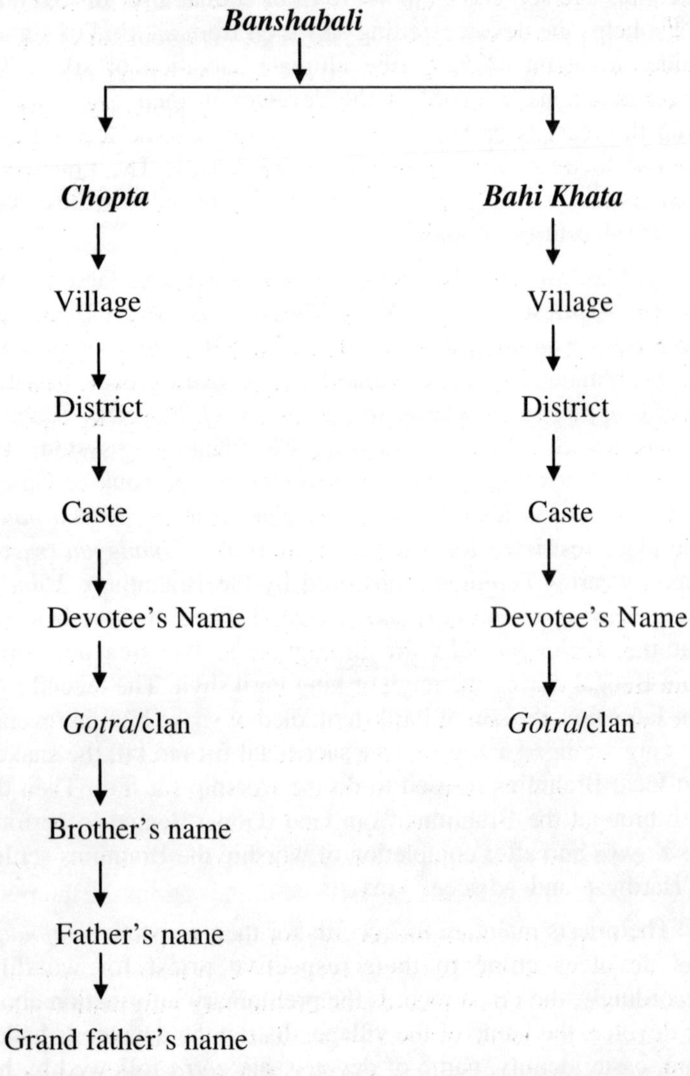

In *Bahi khata*, only the devotee's village name, district name, caste, name of the devotee and his *Gotra* or clan are recorded. In the *bhahi khata* entries of the district and village name are made in alphabetical order so that records can be located easily. In the early days, the records were written on the *Bhoj patra*, the tree bark. Ink was prepared by traditional way. Now-a-days, the modern paper is used for writing. Generally the hard but smooth paper is used. Each of the *khata* is about one meter in length and six inches in width, and is bound with red cloth. All the registers are kept in wooden storage unit. Now-a-days, these genealogical records are used in Courts in cases of land disputes. On receiving letter from Court, the priest forwards the Xerox copies of the documents pertinent to the particular case to the Court. It is also observed that some people come and collect the genealogical records for making family history.

Structural Organisation of *Tirtha Purohit*

The structural Organisation of the *Tirtha Purohit* is known as *Gadhi*. The system of *Gadhi* is the inheritance right of a

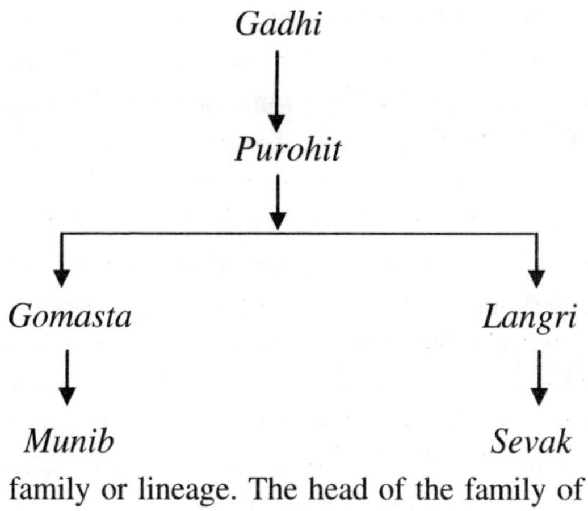

particular family or lineage. The head of the family of the priest maintains the *Gadhi*. After his death the next senior member of the family or his eldest son looks after the *Gadhi*. He is the superior authority of the *Gadhi*. Under his guidance other brothers and rest of service man work. The head of the *Gadhi* is locally known as *Mukhya Purohit*. He supervises and performs worship and welfare of the devotees. The service men are of two categories: *Gomasta* and *Munib*. On the other hand, there are *Langri* and *Sevak*.

The *Gomasta* and *Munib* are involved in a particular *Gadhi* over generations. They got their service through inheritance right and accordingly maintain their *Jajmans*. While *Langri* and *Sevak* get job through recruitment tthere are also people who are associated with a particular *Gadhi* over generations. The *Gomasta*s maintain the *Chopta* and *Bahi khata*. The post of *Gomasta* is generally held by the younger member of the family or lineage of the priest. Sometimes the *Gomasta*s are recruited from outside the family or lineage. The *Munibs* generally maintain account of the *Gadhi* and sometime they also visit *Jajmans* for collection. The *Langri* is to assist the devotees for their welfare. He is to look after the accommodation, railway ticket, food and medical facilities of the devotees. The *Sevak*'s duty is to bring the devotees of the particular *Jajman* and hand them over to the *Gadhi*. The source of income of the *Gadhi* totally depends upon the devotees. On a day, total collection is divided between the owner and other service men proportionately. The *Gadhi* owner gets 75 per cent of the earning while the rest 25 per cent goes to the service men as per their rank like the *Gomasta* receives 10 per cent, *Munib* 10 per cent, *Langri* five per cent and *Sevak* five per cent respectively. Besides, the devotees always give some extra donation in the form of cloth, silver and other materials and also money as Pranami (a token of respect) to the *Gomasta*, *Munib*, *Langri* and *Sevak* in return of their service. In early days, the Zamindar and Aristocrats used to donate huge amount of land, gold, and silver to their priests. It is also observed that some devotees give a huge numbers of cows, coconut tree, ponds, etc., to their priest. The *Munib* or *Gomasta* goes to village and collect money, half yearly or annually.

Structural Organisation of Achariya Maha Brahman Sava

The Achariya Maha Brahman priests trace their migration from Khojra village of Saharanpur discrict. It is told that initially only twenty four families came to Haridwar and settled at Panchapuri area. During those days, twenty four families were engaged in *Karmakanda* worship for twenty four days. Presently Maha Brahman group is having a total of 560 members. Due to increase of family members the Maha Brahman Sava divided their work within the lineage. The Achariya Maha Brahman Sava priests are mainly involved in '*Karmakanda*'. They perform *Sradha*, ancestral worship, etc., which are locally known as *Karmakanda*. The Achariya Brahmin also performs *Karmakanda* for the other Brahmin groups of the place. They are locally known as Maha Brahman because they are *Pindo Dhari* and take *mirthu dhan*, i.e., take cash or kind on occasion of *Sradha*. The Achariya priest does not worship in Ganga temple. The Maha Brahman Sava is a collective organisation and all the Maha Brahman priests are members of the body.

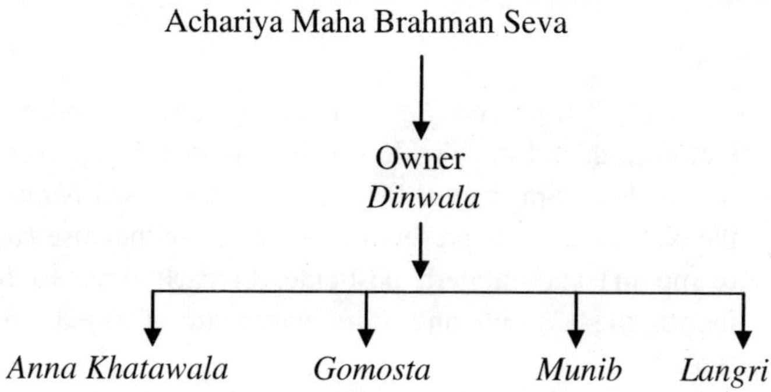

The Achariya Maha Brahman Sava controls the Maha Brahman priests. The president is the supreme authority of the body. He divides the *Pali* (the duties) and other religious activities within the Maha Brahman group. In early days, each of the twenty four families used to get their *Pali* for one day in twenty four days. Now with the increase in number of families the Pali system is arranged accordingly. The records maintaining process is same as earlier as informed by *Tirtha Purohit*. The Maha Brahman also maintains two types of *khata,* i.e., *Chopta* and Bhahi khata. In case of structure of organisation there is difference between the two groups of Brahmins; *Tirtha purohit* maintain *Gadhi* system, i.e., individual ownership but Maha Brahman priests maintain collective organisation. In the Maha Brahman Sava the

Pali system is different from the others groups. President is the highest post. Next post is hold by owner or *Dinwala* who holds the post for only one day. On that day, *Anna Khatawala*, *Gomosta*, *Munib* and *Langri* work under *Dinwala*. Next day, the *Dinwala*, *Anna Khatawala*, *Gomasta*, *Munib* and *Langri* are changed as per *Pali* system. The change is in clockwise. On the particular day, the total collection in cash or kind is divided among the priests as per *Pali* rules and regulation. On the day, the *Dinwala* gets *baro anna,* i.e., three fourh of the earnings and rest four *anna,* i.e., one fourth is divided equally between *Anna khatawala*, *Gomsta*, *Munib*, and *Langri*, each gets *ek anna*, i.e., one share. The *ek anna* share of *Langri* is divided equally between him and his assistant, i.e., *Sevak* and each get *Adha Anna* (half of one share). Besides, the devotees give them individual *Pranami* (a token of reverence) which they enjoy individually.

Preservation

1. All the *Chopta* and *Bahi khata* are covered with red cotton cloth and stack with one after another. It is preserved in wooden storage unit. In early days they used *Nimpata*, the Neem leaves as preservatives; presently they use *kapur* (camphor) and modern pesticide. In each three to four month the *Chopta* and *Bahi khata* are warmed up in sunlight.
2. In early days, the people used a mixture of *Neem pati* dust and *Kapur* as pesticide which was spread over the *Bhoga patra*.

Bhog Patra

Bhog patra is a type of tree available in the area. The priest used to collect the tree bark, cleaned and dried it in the sun light for three to four days. The dried up barks were cut into pieces as per their requirement. Then they used to make a bundle and keep in a dry place. The *Bhog patra* is locally known as *Bhoga bhasha*, which is available in *Bhoga bhasha* Jungle near Badrinath and Gongotri area.

Preparation of Ink

In early days, the priest used to make ink in traditional way. Ink is called *kali*. It takes a long process for preparation and its materials were collected from natural surroundings. The preparation for ink used to begin with collection of earthen pot. The pot was generally having three or four sear capacity; the ink makers occasionally used metal pot also. Water was collected from banana tree by pushing a half round shaped piece of bamboo or iron through its stem part and below the channel a pot was kept for storing water. It used to take seven or eight hours to get one pot full of water. This collected water was mixed up with khayer dust in a proportion of 1:3, i.e., one shear khayer mixed with two shear water. The mixed khayer water was boiled for three to four hours. Before that, the maker prepares *kali*. The banana leaves smeared with mastered oil were held over the lit oil lamp and as a result black *kali* appeared on the leaves. Sometime metal plates were used for in lieu of banana leaves. The prepared *kali* was then mixed with the liquid mixture. In the next stage they used to make glue like paste from Sonamukhi fruits. Such kind of glue is still used by the local people. Then all these items (the *kali* prepared of oil, Sonamukhi paste) and Sohaga khil were mixed with the liquid in the earthen pot. It was then boiled again for two to three hours and kept in the sun light for few hours. This final product became ink for writing. After three or four months the ink was to keep in sun light for preservation.

Traditional Pen

Traditionally people used to make their pen from bamboo. The senior or influential people used feather of peacock for the purpose.

Taboos

The priests observe some rules and regulation in their social and religious life. In Indian society there are certain occasions when a period of pollution is observed and certain norms are maintained. The *Tirtha purohit*, of Haridwar remains absent from worship during such occasions.

Shutak, the birth pollution: On the birth of a child three days pollution period is observed for all the family members. The period ends with a purification ceremony along with a *puja* (worship).

Patak, the death pollution: on occurrence of a death in a family ten days pollution period is observed and the priests do not perform any worship. On eleventh day a rite is performed where some Brahmins along with *Kulaguru* are ceremonially offered with a feast (Brahmin bhojan). After this they are allowed to perform the worship. During his period of absence from worship the priest makes a mutual arrangement with some other priests who performs the duties on his behalf. This is called thika system.

Mashik dharma, menstruation cycle: During the menstruation cycle of his wife the priest does not participate in any worships. If any emergency arises the priest borrows other priest to perform on his behalf.

The Priest

As Haridwar is a place of religious repute, Brahmins, the priestly caste of Hindu society, came to this place at different times. Besides, the other people like Barber, sweeper or Safaiyala, Milkmen etc. also came to the place and devoted their labour in different ways. The Brahmins of Hardwar have further classification within the group on the basis of their division of work, allotted by the Brahma Samaj and later on by the Ganga Sava committee. Earlier there was a category of Rajguru Brahmin who used to serve the royal families. The *Kula Purohit* is socially occupying higher position in the Brahmin society. He is also engaged by other Brahmin groups of the area for worship. Besides, he participates in *Sanskar* and *Upanayan*. The *Tirtha Purohits* are the dominant Brahmin groups of Haridwar. They are involved in *Sanskar*, *Upanayan*, *Mundan* and Ganga Worship activities. Now-a-days, there are about 2,500 families of *Tirtha Purohit* in Haridwar. They play a major role in temple activities. All the activities of the temple are performed by the *Tirtha Purohits*. The Ganga Sava committee and other administrative power are also held by the *Tirtha Purohit* priests.

Maha Brahmans, also known as Achariya Maha Brahmans are the second largest group of priests in Haridwar. They are generally engaged in *Karmakanda,* i.e., *Sradha* and ancestral worship. The Maha Brahman priest belongs to lower group of priests within the Brahmin society. According to other Brahmin groups the Maha Brahman group is assigned with lower status as they accepts *Pindo* and earn money from that.

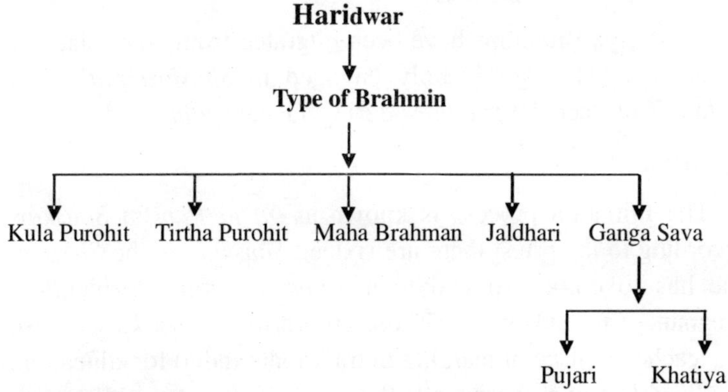

Pujari Khatiya

The Jaldhari Brahmin is mainly engaged for water supply during the ancestral worship, *Sradha*, *Upanayan*, *Sanaskar,* etc. The Jaldhari Brahmins perform their work on temporary basis. They have no right to deal with *Jajmani* system. Their source of income depends on the devotee's donation.

Ganga Sava priests are mainly of two types: *Pujari* and Khatiya. *Pujaris* are appointed by the Ganga Sava committee. This is contractual service for a period of four years. The Ganga *Pujari* compulsorily belongs to *Tirtha Purohit* group. The other groups of priests are not entitled for performing the Ganga worship. He is assisted by two or three groups of assistant *pujari* who help him in arranging flower, prasad, milk, etc., for the worship. In the evening, the other *pujari* groups are mainly involved for 'arati'. It is a huge activity at *Har-ki-pauri*. The thousands of devotees every day offer 'Dwiya' (the traditional ritual lamp) to Ganga Mata for her well-wishes. The *Pujari* receives monthly salary from Ganga Sava committee and his other source of income is from the devotee's *pranami*. The total collection of *Pranami* is divided equally between the Ganga Sava and the *Pujari*.

The Khatiya Brahman, also known as Ghat Brahman, migrates from other places mainly season wise. They perform Ganga *puja* outside the temple for the tourists and put *tika* (holy mark) on the forehead of the devotees. They sit on Ganga ghat only on permission from *Tirtha Purohit* as the place has been occupied by the *Tirtha Purohit* since long. The day's income is equally shared with *Tirtha Purohit*.

Shashtriya Brahmins have been migrated from other place of the country. They are mainly engaged in *Shashra path,* i.e., recitation of sacred scriptures during Ganga *puja*.

Initiation

The Initiation process is known as *Yayja Pabitra Sanskar*. According to the priest there are sixteen *Sanskars* in the *Shastra*. One has to come cross sixteen *Sanskars* from *Garbhadhan* (pregnancy) to end of life. There are various *Guru kuls* (house of a teacher, a place of learning in traditional India) for education. In *Guru kul* one learns all *Puranas*, *Vedas*, as well as all procedures of worship. The *Yayja Pabitra Sanskar* day is generally preferred on *Baishakhi panchami*, i.e., the fifth lunar day of the month of *Baishakh* (April-May). On the day, the *Kula Guru* performs the worship. The disciple should take a holy dip, wear new cloth, undergo *mundane*, put on a new sacred thread and finally gets *guru mantra*. Then he becomes entitled to perform worship.

Religious Belief and Practices

Haridwar is one of the great centres of Hindu pilgrimage in India. The major religious celebrations include the worship on the occasions of solar and lunar eclipses, *Kartik-purnima* (the full moon day in the month of *Kartik*), *Makar Sankranti*, *Vikhauti*, *Jeth Dasahra*, *Somwati Amavasya*, the *Kumbha* and *Ardha Kumbha* etc. Some routine worship is as follows:

Ganga Puja: The Ganga worship is performed as daily rituals as well as annually. The daily worship includes *Pratho arati*,

Madhyan arati and *Shayan-kal arati*. The *puja* is performed by the chief *Pujari*.

Pratho arati: The *Pratho Arati* starts early in the morning. In this time other *pujari* performs *arati*. Offerings include milk, flowers, and a mixture of *curd*, honey and Ghee, known as *Charnamrita*. The fruits offered are banana, apple and coconut. After *puja Charnamritha* and *Prasad* (the sanctified food of the god) is distributed among all the devotees.

Madhyan arati: The *Madhyan Arati puja* is scheduled to mid-day. The head and assistant *Pujari* perform *arati* respectively. During *Madhyan Arati*, *Suji*, *ghee*, *puri* and *khir* form the food of the god. After *puja prasad* is distributed among the devotees.

Shayan–kal arati: The *Shayan-kal arati* is performed in the evening. Arati is performed by the priest. A huge crowd of devotees attend the occasion and offer *dwiya*. Offerings to the deity include *suji, ghee, puri* and *khir*.

Annual Worship

Ganga Saptami: In the month of *Baishakh*, on the seventh day (Saptami) of the bright fortnight, Ganga is worshipped. The day is believed to be the birth day of mother goddess Ganga. On the day only milk and curd is offered to the deity.

Dashaki Ganga: The *Dashaki Ganga* is celebrated on the tenth day of *Sukla-paksha* (bright fortnight), in the month of *Jaistha*. The day is marked with the arrival of goddess Ganga at Haridwar. On the day the devotees offer milk and special rice locally known as Sarbati rice to the deity.

Ganga Sava: During the British period, the British Government took major steps for better irrigation facilities. As a result, work was initiated for a proposed Yamuna and Ganga canals. In 1839, Colonel P. Cautley undertook a survey of the area. In the year of 1913 the canal work started. In 1914, there was a revolt from the local people against the canal. In 1916, Sri Madan Mohan Malviya, *Tirtha Purohit* of Haridwar along with Sree Mahano Shadhu group took up the leadership and formed Ganga Sava

Samiti. Since then Ganga Sava looks after administration, religious activities and welfare of devotees.

The Ganga Sava is a self administered religious organisation. The working committee is formed by election. The voting right for Ganga Sava follows two criteria, one, the voter must belong to *Tirtha Purohit* group and second, he should belong to Dhara panchyat which is restricted to mainly five villages, i.e., Panchapuri which consists of five villages like Haridwar, Jawlapur Kankhal, Khar khari and Bhimgura.

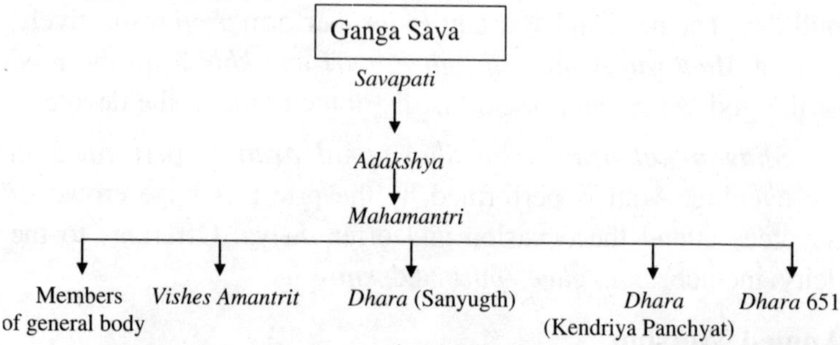

Tirtha Purohit voters: According to by-law of the Ganga Sava, only the *Tirtha Purohits* enjoy the voting right among the priest groups. The *Tirtha Purohit* group is having 650 voters presently. They follow certain norm to select the voters e.g. the families having one to five family members contribute one voter each, familics having one to 10 members contribute two voters each and the families having more than 10 members contribute three voters each, which is the maximum number of voters from a family. The family members mutually select the knowledgeable person from the family as voter.

Dhara Panchyat voters: It is said that, during the days of King's ruling devotees used to donate land and movable wealth for temple. Those properties are enjoyed by the priests for their own self a well as for the temple activities. In addition they also take part in the Ganga Sava. As per norm there are representation from *Dhara* (3 members), *Dhara Sanyugth* (3 members) and *Dhara Kendriya Panchyat* (3 members) to the Ganga Sava.

The *Dhara* families select knowledgeable persons as their candidates.

Vishes Amantrit: There are altogether 11 members as *Vishes Amantrit* (specially invited guests).

The Ganga Sava body consists of *Savapati* (President), *Adhakshya* (Speaker, second in position) and by *Mahamantri* (Prime minister, third in position). The post of *Savapati* is the highest position in the body. He selects 11 *Vishes Amantrit* members of the body; such members are highly qualified like Doctors, Lawyer, and Journalist etc. They mainly suggest new ideas for running the Ganga Sava. The *Adhakshya* conducts general meetings and emergency meetings. The *Mahamantri* though third in position in the body but he holds maximum power of the body. He supervises the activities of the body and is answerable for any problems. The general members from *Tirtha Purohit* (650), the *Dhara* members (9) finally select *Savapati*, *Adakshya* and *Mahamantri* through secret ballot. *Mahamantri* is empowered to select other *Mantris* for different departments in support of *Savapati* and *Adakshya*. The duration of the Ganga Sava body is of four years.

The Ganga Sava was established with the objective of providing comfort and facilities to pilgrims and to maintain purity and dignity of the holy place. Its main function is to maintain hygienic condition around the *Har-ki-pauri* area, restoring lost children, disposal of unclaimed dead bodies and immersion of ashes in the Ganga sent by the people from far and wide and to guide the pilgrims visiting holy places of Pancha-puri. It also runs a library and a dispensary which provides free medical aid to the pilgrims and poor. The volunteers of this organisation do useful work in the *mela* (fair) by extending every kind of help to the needy. They are posted on ghats for traffic control and for maintaining law and order. On such occasions they also supply rations to the pilgrims. The Sava arranges for the performance of *arti*, recitation of *katha* and maintenance of spiritual atmosphere of the place undisturbed.

Besides, there are some other welfare organisations active in Haridwar. The Seva Samiti was established by Dr Pitamber Das Pant in 1919 with the objective of serving devotees. The main function of the Samiti is similar to that of the Ganga Sava. The Bharat Seva Sangh was established in 1919 by Swami Yoganandaji for rendering social service by way of running a charitable dispensary and thus helping the sick and the needy. Shri Sanatan Dharma Punjab Mahabir Dal was established in 1931. The organisation was greatly influenced by Sri Madan Mohan Malviya. It sought to attract an increasing participation of youth in social and religious activities. Besides looking after the improvement of the temple and other religious places, the Dal undertakes relief operation at the time of fairs and religious gatherings. The Suraj Sewa Dal, Manglaur, was founded in 1965 by Nand kishor Sharma and M.M Jain to help the poor and the needy.

Observation

From the above disussions, it is clear that people are very closely attached to their religious mind-set. The religious activity is a life line of the human being. On the other hand, centering the sacred place a *jajmani* relationship is built between the priests and the devotees. Such relationship involves economic dependency as well social status and social values, which makes a social order of the society. The whole process generates rich traditional knowledge that transmits over generations. At the same time a rich cultural heritage is maintained from generation to generation. Due to impact of tourism the traditional occupation gradually threats their economic condition. So, the time is calling for help to preserve the data based records for feature generation.

Acknowledgement

First and foremost, I wish to offer my heartfelt thanks to Dr V. R. Rao, former Director-in-Charge, Anthropological Survey of India, for the facilities, supports and encouragement that he had extended to me all through. I also express my sincere gratitude to Prof K.K. Misra, Director, Anthropological Survey of India, for his inspiration and initiative to publish this study. My profound thanks to the Administrative body of the Shri Shri Ganga registered committee, Haridwar for their cooperation. They extended their support in every respect during my field work. I am grateful to Pt Sanjay Chakrawarti and Pt Rajiv Chakrawarti (Ram Ghat) for their valuable suggestions related to project work. I am also equally indebted to Shri S. Shatri and the entire Kush ghat Pt Maha Sava committee. They extended all possible help and cooperation to make this study a success. I am equally obliged to Dr K Chakrabarty (P.I) and Head of Office, Anthropological Survey of India, Eastern Regional Centre, Kolkata, Dr K. Mandal and Smt, K. Basu, Eastern Regional Centre, Kolkata for their valuable suggestions to make a good report.

References

Fonin, K.S. (1977). Uttarakhanda, Garhwal, Himalayas. Asian Journal, Derhadun.

Kamal K. Misra (2005). Indegenous Knowledge, Natural Resource Management and Development: The Konda Reddy Experience, Bhopal and New Delhi: IGRS, Pratibha Prakashan.

Swami Sivananda (1994) Mother Ganga. Published by The Divine Life Society. Distt. Tehri-Garhwal. U.P., Himalayas, India.

Varun, D.P (1980). 'Uttar Pradesh District' Gazetteers, Saharanpur. Government of U.P.

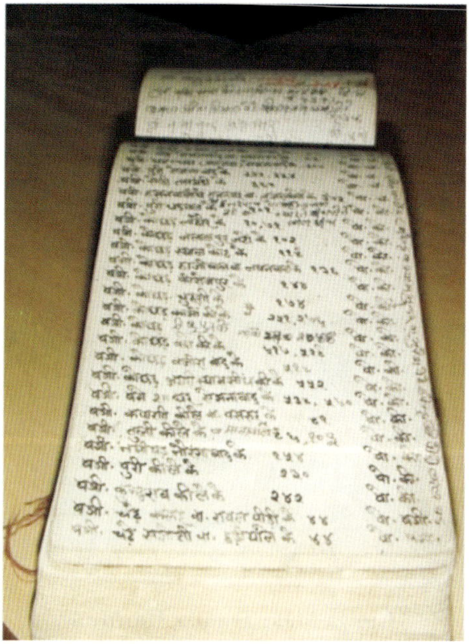

***Banshabali* (Genealogical Record Book), Haridwar.**

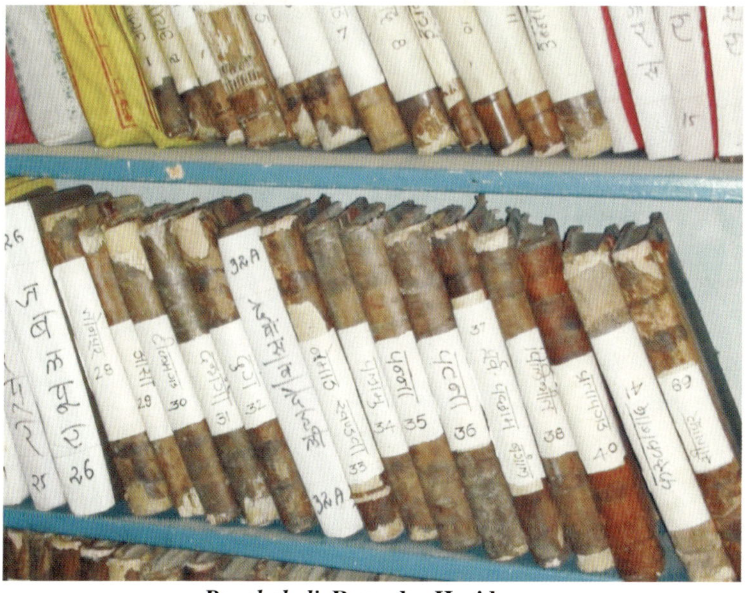

***Banshabali* Records, Haridwar.**

Ganga Mata Temple, Haridwar.

Priests Recording *Banshabali* of the Devotees, Haridwar.

Devotees Performing Ancestral Worship, Haridwar.

Worshipping Ganga, Haridwar.

View of *Har-ki-Pauri*, Haridwar.

Devotees Performing Worship at Haridwar.

3

Genealogical Records and Traditional Knowledge System: A Study of Kamakhya Temple

Krishna Mandal and *Krishna Basu*

Introduction

The Kamakhya temple, also known as Mahashaktipith, is one of the most important and famous sacred centre for pilgrimage under the doctrine of Hinduism in India. It is situated on the Nilachal hill at the height of 525 feet on the western part of Guwahati city in the state of Assam, the ancient Kamrup State. The River Brahmaputra flows through its northern side.

The importance of Kamakhya temple has its root in Indian mythology. It recognises Kamakhya as one of the 51 pithas (sacred centre) where one of the bodily parts of Sati, the consort of Lord Siva, was fallen. According to *Kalika Purana*, the ancient sacred scripture, the story goes like this: once King Dakshya, the father of Sati, performed a *yagna* (the sacrificial fire), where he did not invite his daughter and son-in-law. It was an intentional insult to lord Siva by the king. Sati could not accept such behaviour from her father and decided to attend the occasion at her parental house. When Sati arrived at the place, king Dakshya started abusing Siva as he was unhappy with his son-in-law. Sati could not tolerate the insult of her husband and parted with her life on the spot. With the news of Sati's demise, Siva lost his patience.

He immediately rushed to the place and started *tandava* (frantic) dance carrying the lifeless body of Sati on his shoulder. The earth started shaken with the anger of Siva and it was going to be destroyed. To save the earth from destruction lord Vishnu applied his *chakra* (Vishnu's discus) to cut Satis body into pieces to make it parted with lord Siva. It is believed that Sati's body was cut into fiftyone pieces each of which was fallen in different parts of the country. Each of these places was revered as Sakti-pitha or Sati-pitha, the sacred centre of Sati/Sakti-cult, i.e., the cult of mother goddess. The popular belief is that Mahamudra Yoni, i.e., the reproductive organ of Sati was fallen on the Neelachal hill of ancient Assam named Kamrup. The mountain represented the body of Siva and when Sati's genital organ fell on it, the mountain turned blue, thus, called Neelachal, i.e., Blue Mountain (neel=blue, achal=mountain).

According to legend the goddess (Sati, a form of goddess Durga) is called Kamakhya here because she came there secretly to satisfy her amour (*kama*) with Siva. Thus the source of *Kalika Purana* makes the mountain both a grave-yard and a secret love-tryst of the Goddess. Within the temple there is a cave, in a corner of which stands a block of stone on which the symbol of a *Yoni* has been sculptured. The stone remains moist from the oozing of a natural spring within the cave. The offerings of flowers and leaves are made on the *Yoni*. It is believed that worship of Kamakhya grants *moksha*, the ultimate spiritual release. Under Tantric cult Kamakhya was identified with Kali, the cult of Sakti, the essence of female energy. So, in all other respects, i.e., the daily rites and ceremonies Goddess Kali is worshipped with sacrifices of animals. The devotees offer scarifice to mother Goddess according to their desire. The *Kalika Purana* describes Kamakhya as the yielder of all desires and the giver of salvation.

The place earned high reputation among the sakti-pitha and therefore regarded as *maha* (great) sakti-pitha. There are other stories also regarding the origin and significance of Kamakhya (see appendix). The temple is having 40000 bighas of land under its possession which are called Debottar, i.e., the property belongs to the deity. All the Debottar lands are located in Jhalukbari mouza under P.S named so. It is one of the great religious places of India since ancient times. Pilgrims from various places of India as well as from the neighbouring countries of Bangladesh and Nepal visit this temple since olden days. There are many *kimbadanti* (myths, legend, sayings etc.) about the Tantric worship of this temple; the temple occupied a very significant place in the gamut of Tantric worship in India and abroad. There are a number of temples encircling the main temple of Kamakhya; of them ten temples are dedicated to Dasamahavidya, i.e., ten forms of goddess Durga, namely Kali, Tara, Soroshi, Bhubaneswari, Bhairabi, Chinnyamasta, Dhumabati, Bagala, Matangi (Saraswati), Kamala (Lakshmi) and rest are dedicated to the different forms (*rupa*) of Lord Siva such as Kameswar, Siddheswar, Kotilinga, Aaghore and Amraketswar.

According to a myth the original temple of goddess Kamakhya was built by Kamdev, the God of lust with the help of celestial architect Vishwakarma. It is said that Kamdev was turned to ashes by Shiva for obstructing his meditation. He regained life and beauty when he promised to built the temple, hence the name Kamakhya or Kamrup.

Historically it is said that the Kamakhya temple was destroyed by Kalapahar, the Muslim invader and thereafter it was reconstructed by Naranarayana, the Koch King of Koch Bihar in 1665 A.D. The King brought Brahmins from Purba Banga, the then East Bengal (now Bangladesh) for the worship of goddess Kamakhya and donated land to them (Brahmmattor) to settle down. The king also donated lands for the maintenance of the *sevaks* (the servitor to the god) of the temple (Kha Chaudhury, Amanatulla Ahmed: 1936 (rep. 1990) Koch Biharer Itihash, (in Bengali, p. 127).

Various groups of people are directly or indirectly involved in different activities of this temple. From the inception of this temple a system was introduced for recording of some basic information about the pilgrims who were hailed from various places. The duty of recording information was allotted to the Brahmin *sevaks* of the deity, living in the temple complex. The responsibility was succeeded from generation to generation. Therefore such records were also updated with the information of the descending generation. The updated records of the pilgrims are being maintained by the temple authority for their own working system. From the systematic maintenance of records, genealogical information of the pilgrims is known.

In the Kamakhya Temple genealogical records, locally known as *banshabali*, is maintained by Brahmin servitors who are known as Pandā as well as Bardeori and Nanandeori. The record book is locally known as *Yatrik/Jatrik khata* (Yatri/Jatri=pilgrim/devotee; khata=note-book). The Brahmins who have been worshipping the goddess Kamakhya are called Bardeoris and the Brahmins who have been worshipping deities around the Kamakhya Temple are called Nanan deoris/Nandeori.

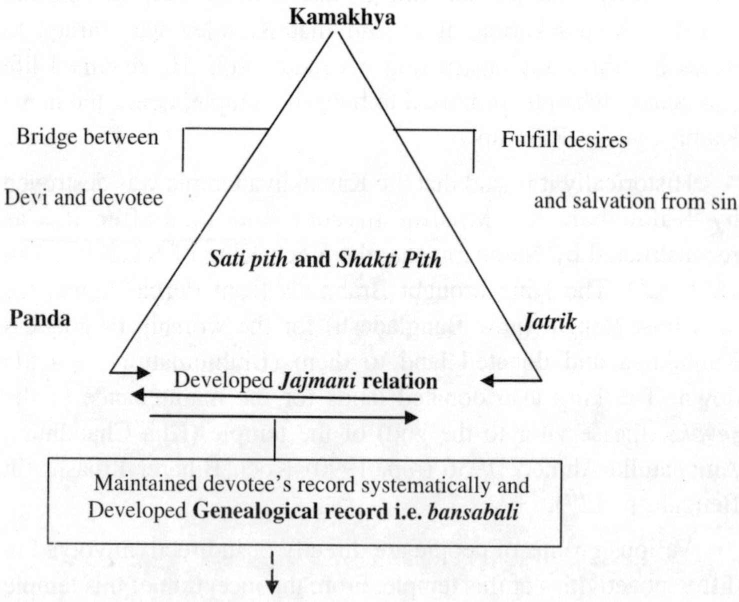

The above diagram shows, over the passage of time how the religious belief system has developed around the temple. The beliefs around Kamakhya temple is mainly based on two inspirations, i.e., *Sati pith* and *Shakti pith*. The devotees come and worship here to fulfill the individual or family's desire and to achieve salvation from sin. On the other hand, the Tantric group comes to acquire power of penance. The Brahmans or Pandā are the media for the devotees to reach their goal through worshiping the deities. Such interactions facilitate a reciprocal relation between the priest and devotees, better called as *Jajmani*. The priest, apart from religious rites also maintains the records of the *jajmans*. The process of record maintenance involves traditional knowledge. In Kamakhya temple the genealogical records, the *bansabali*, are maintained in *Yatrik khata*.

The present study intended to probe into the process of how the Brahmin *sevayats/sevaks* of the Kamakhya temple are recording, maintaining and preserving the records of *bansabali* in a traditional way. The standard anthropological tools and techniques have been applied to collect data. Empirical data were collected from Burha, Deka, Bidhipathak and Hota of Bardeori group of Brahmin, from Chandi-pathak, i.e., the Brahmin *sevak* who recites chandi (the sacred book describing the glory of goddess Chandi) at the time of worship of Kamakhya and from Nanan *pujaris/* Nanandeoris who perform *puja* (worship) at *nanan Devalaya* (other temples; *nanan*=other; *devalaya*=temples), i.e., the temples other than that of Kamakhya.

The Structural Organisation of Priest and the Record Maintaining System

It was told that about one hundred Brahmans were brought to Kamrupa by Bhagadutta, one of the Rulers, for performing Vedic rites. In later times Bengali Brahmans were invited by the then king Rudra Singha. Over the time the temple complex of Kamakhya remained under the patronage of the rulers who controlled the functions and the functionaries of the temple. For management of the priestly services Brahmins were brought from different parts of the country, mainly from Kanauj, Mithila and Bengal or Banga. The Ahom kings gave rent free land to them for their survival and service to the temples duties. A deed of gift inscribed on the copper plate was issued to the Brahmins from the part of the kings. In later years Rudra Singha, one of the great Ahom kings brought a famous Tantric namely Krishnaram Bhattacherjee from a village of Santipur, now West Bengal to get himself consecrated to Saktism and appointed him as the *Kula Guru*, the family preceptor of the Ahom kings. But, the king died before his consecration in 1714 and after his death his son Siba Singha along with his wife consecrated to Saktism and fulfilled the wish of his father. He placed *Kulaguru* in the hill of Neelachal with huge landed property to look after the Temple. The Bhattacherjee priest was known as *Parbatia Gosain* and was accepted as their *Guru,* i.e., the spiritual teacher (Sharma, Ganga: 1978, pp. 57-58). The other Brahmin groups were assigned with various temple duties. The following diagram shows work assignments of the Brahmins and classification of work. This classification of work facilitated an internal hierarchical system among the Brahmins.

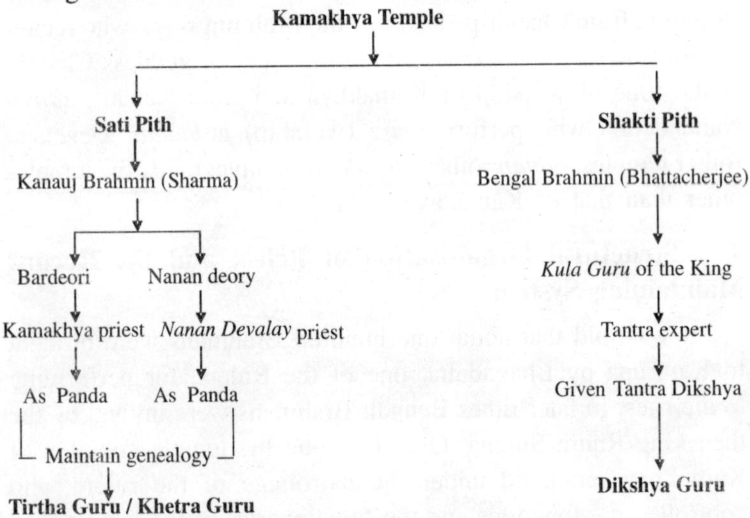

The priests were mainly divided into two categories: *Tirtha guru* or *Khetra guru* and *Dikshya guru* or *Raj Kulo guru*. The *Tirtha Gurus* belong to Kanauj Brahmin and they use 'Sharma' as title. *Tirtha gurus* are further classified into two groups namely

Bardeori and *Nanan deori*. The Bardeoris perform priestly work in the Kamakhya temple like daily *puja* (*nittya puja*), festivals, and special ceremonies of the temple. They are also called Barpujari. The Nanandeoris are the priests for Daso Mahabidya Temples, locally known as *Nanan devalay*. The priests for *Nanan devalay* are locally known as *Nanandeori*. Both the groups of priest maintain *Jatrik Khata* through which they maintain the *jajmani* relations with the devotees. Whenever a devotee (jajman) comes to Kamakhya for pilgrimage he or she stays with their family *Pandā's* house and in return the devotee donates in cash or kind as *dakshina/pranami,* i.e., the honourarium as a mark of reverence.

The cooks of Kamakhya temple is locally known as *khoar* Brahmin. The Chandipathak and *khoar* Brahmin of the Kamakhya temple are included in the *nanan devalay* priest. These two categories of Brahmins are not directly involved with Kamakhya temple, i.e., they have no right to *Nittya puja* of the Kamakhya temple but enjoy right to worship at temple dedicated to Daso Mahavidya. The Bardeori priests look after all the activities of Kamakhya temple. Due to increase of population, both these priest groups introduced *pali* system to regulate the service to the deities. '*Pali*' is a work distribution system within the allocated rotation of duties of the priests. All Brahmins of the Kamakhya temple and Daso Mahavidya temple maintain records of the devotees (*Jatrik*) since a long time. It may be said here both the groups of priests are referred to as 'Pandā' by the devotees.

Traditional Knowledge

According to Webster's Dictionary, Traditional Knowledge means the knowledge communicated from ancestors to descendants by word only, transmitted from age to age without writing, as traditional options, traditional customs and traditional expositions of the scriptures. It is also meant observant of tradition attached to old customs (Source: Internet). Traditional Knowledge comprises the 'knowledge' innovations and a practice of the indigenous and local communities around the world, which is developed from experience, gained over centuries and adapted to the local culture and environment, and is transmitted orally from generation to generation.

In the Kamakhya Temple, the Brahmin priests (sevak), i.e., the Bardeories and Nanandeories have been maintaining the genealogical record book or *yatrik khata* since olden times. The *Jatrik Khata* is of two types: *Asol khata* (original record book) and *Nakol khata* (the copied book). Regarding the knowledge and technique of record writing, they have learnt it from their older generations and passed it to their new generations. For the maintenance of the records they used to follow the traditional technique. In the bygone days, the priests used to prepare ink and pen in their own way, from local available resource.

In olden days, the bark of khasi tree or sanchi tree was used as writing materials (pat) and the pen was made of khagra wood. For writing on the thin layers of Khasi or Sanchi tree (called khasi pat or sanchi pat) they used to prepare ink from powder of haritaki (Myrobalan fruits) mixing with soot (jhul) of kitchen, urine of cows and dews.

Preparation of Khasi Pat or Sanchi Pat

First the thin layers from khasi bark were taken out and kept in water for five days. The process removes its inner particles and makes it soft. Then these soften layers were kept under the sun for drying up. To avoid shrinking of the pat while drying, ten to fifteen such pats were placed together one upon another and some weight were placed on the top. Lastly haritaki, was to make them smooth. With the advancement of technology, paper came into use in place of khasi pat or sanchi pat.

When pilgrims come to the temple for performing the puja, the respective Pandā (priest) records their names in the *Asol khata*, the entry register. The other information about the devotee required to be recorded are—his village, district and post office, name of his father, date of visit to the temple and his *gotra,* etc. Later on the respective Pandā transfer the record from *Asol khata* to *Nakol khata*. Recording order is like this: name of the devotee, his father's name, name of the village, name of the post office, *gotra* and date. While transferring records from *Asol Khata* to *Nakol Khata* the priest enters the data district wise so that the record can be located at any moment at ease. In *Asol khata* devotee's signature is compulsorily taken.

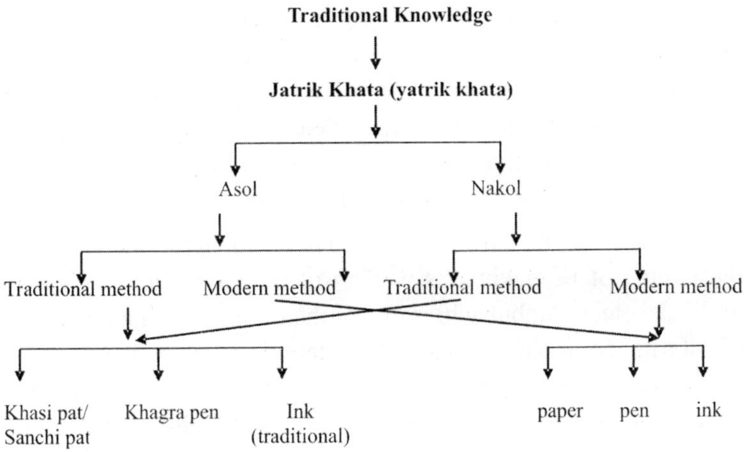

Pagination: Both *Asol* and *Nakol khata* are properly paginated by the Pandās. In *Nakol khata* further indexing is done district wise. For example, indexing would come like this: Khulna district page 1 to 10, Faridpur district 11 to 15, Dacca district 16 to 30 and so on. When data is copied down from *Asol Khata* to *Nakol khata* page number of *Asol khata* where the actual entry was made is also noted down.

Jajmani Relation

The word '*Jajmani*' originally derives from the Sanskrit term '*Jajamana*' means sacrificial patron who employs priests for a ritual. It is told that previously the Pandās used to visit their *jajmans* in various corners of the country like West Bengal (district of Burdwan, Birbhum, Darjeeling and the city of Kolkata), Assam, Uttar Pradesh, Bihar, North-eastern States and even the neighbouring country of Bangladesh. They used to travel in a group of two to three persons. About fifty years ago they used to visit Calcutta (now Kolkata) at a regular interval and stayed at Bata Krishna Paul's house and also at other places to make contact with their *jajmans*. Sometimes in distress the *jajmans* were given money by the priests as loan and during their visit the Pandās used to recover the loans from them and also invited them (devotees) for coming to Kamakhya on the occasion of Ambubachi, and other festivities like Durga Puja, Manasa Puja etc. When the Pandās had less work in their hand at that time they had to stay in Kolkata for one or two months. For this the Pandā had to pay Rs. 11 (rupees eleven) only as room rent. There was a big hall at Paul's house for cooking for the Pandās. Cook was there for the service of the guests.

Pandās are the *Tirtha Gurus*. They propagate the glory of the temple of Kamakhya as well as of the Gods and Goddesses to the devotees. Ambubachi is one of the most important occasions of pilgrimage at Kamakhya and the temple receives huge crowd of devotees. The priests keep regular contact with the *jajmans*. Earlier the *jajmani* relationship was strong and often the well-off people (*jajmans*) donated gold, land, house and money to the Pandās against their services. Now the *Jajmani* relation is not as strong as of the old days. With the development of Telecommunication system especially the mobile/cell phone correspondence between the priest and the *jajmans* became easy nowadays. The *khatas* are also not maintained strictly. Now often the Pandās record addresses of their *jajmans* in mobile phone. The devotees also often prefer to stay in hotels at Guwahati. From the hotels they contact to their respective Pandā over telephone. The panda collects the entry tickets for the *jajmans* and takes them to the temple for *darshan* and *pujas*. Previously there was no ticket system for *darshan* (to see) to the goddess Kamakhya. It has been introduced by the Kamakhya Debottar Board since 2004. There are different categories of tickets: a special ticket costs Rs.501, a part special ticket costs Rs.101, for personnel from military service ticket costs Rs. 10/- only. For performing any *mangalik anusthan* (auspicious rites) at the temple like marriage registration etc. the temple committee charges Rs. 41 only from the devotees and the members of Kamakhya Temple.

Sevapuja and *Sevaks*: Historicity and Development

Regarding the dating of Kamakhya temple, there is difference of opinions among the scholars. According to Pratap Barapujari that Kamakhya temple was popularised since the rise of Koch dynasty in 16th century A.D. In his article 'Kalapahar and Kamakshya Temple' (JARS, Vol. IV, No. 2, 1936, pp. 42-46) Nath said that a large section of devotees still believe that iconoclast Kalapahar who led an invasion of Kamarupa was responsible for the destruction of the temple. While Sastri, opines that the Kamakhya temple faced its ruin on account of natural calamities like earthquake (JARS, Vol. XIV, 1979-80, pp. 6-7). The two stone inscriptions at the entrance chamber of the main shrine read that king Malladeva and his brother Sukladhaja built the temple in Saka 1487, i.e., 1565 A.D. (Neog, 2001).

Kamrup was ruled by the king of various dynasties in different times like Mahiranga, Naraka, Bhagadatta, Gupta, Barmans, Mlechas, Palas, Mughals and Ahoms. It is Ahom kings who had contributed positively for the development of the Temples in Assam, especially the temples of Kamakhya. Ahom, a section of the Tai people from Southern China entered Kamrupa through south-eastern part of Brahma Putra valley. The Ahom king Cakradharsimha and his several successors were the followers of Vaisnavism. However king Gadadharsimha who ascended the throne in 1681 A.D. was a Saiva (the worshipper of Lord Siva) and reconstructed the Saiva temple at Umananda in the midst of Brahmmaputra River. His son and successor Rudrasimha (1698-1714) was a great patron of Hinduism. He continued the practice of granting extensive area of land and a number of men for regular worship and maintenance of the temple. He made liberal donations to the Brahmins. Rudrasimha invited Krisnaram Nyayabagis from Shantipur (in district Nadia of West Bengal) and was given the charge of Kamakhya temple. He was a Tantric Sākta (sākta=the worshipper of Sakti, the energy in the form of female). Some people were also appointed for *Sevapuja* (worship through service to the deities); they were called *Sevaka* or Pandā. His son and successor Sivasimha (1714 -1744 A.D.) received his initiation from Krishnaram. Thus Saktism gained high favour from Sivasimha. Almost all the shrines of Kamrup received grants of land and *Sevaka* from him (Adhikary: 2001, pp. 8-14A).

In Kamakhya worship is performed in two methods: Tantrik and Baidik. Both have a common base: the *yagna/hom*, *Ghata Sthapana* (installation of earthen water-pot for worshipping it as the symbolic representation of certain deity) and the *puja padhyati* (the method of worship). The *puja* of the goddess Kamakhya is done with *sorosh upachar* (sixteen items).

Functionaries (*Sevakas*) of the Temple

There are a number of functionaries who have different roles in the sacred performances of the temple. There are two categories of *sevakas* associated with the Kamakhya Temple, viz., Brahmins and the non-Brahmins. The Brahmin category includes priests (Bardeori/Barapujari and Nanandeori/Nanan pujari) and the cooks, i.e., *khoar* Brahmins.

Again Bardeoris/Bara *pujaris* are divided into five categories namely Burha, Deka, Hota, Bidhipathak and Brahma. They have hereditary rights of performing *Nittya Puja* (daily worship) of goddess Kamakhya. Their title is Sarma. They believed to be hailed from Kanuj. They, if situation demands, can also worship the Gods and Goddesses of *Nanan Devalaya.*

The *Nanan pujaris/Nanan Nanandeoris* have only rights of performing *pujas* of the God and Goddesses at *Nanan Devalaya*, i.e., the Dasomahavidya temples (comprising the temples of Kali, Tara, Soroshi, Chinnyamastya, Dhumaboti, Bhubaneswari, Bagala Matangi, Kamala). Their title is also Sarma and they also claimed to have come from Kanuj. Besides, there are Chandipathaks. To become a priest of the Kamakhya temple, one has to receive *Dikshya* (consecration) from *Dikshya guru.*

Work of *Bardeori* (clan wise)

Type of Brahmin -	Buhra	Deka	Brahma	Hota	Bidhipathak
Work of Brahmin	Pujari	Pujari	Chanting hymns	Havon	Recite Bidhi /Shastriya
Clan group	Kashyap	Kashyap	Bhargav/ Bharadwaj	Bhargav	Kashyap

To maintain the *nittya pujas* there is a system of daily turn which is known as *pala* or *pali*. Previously it was not present. During the reign of Gadadharsimha the *pali* system run as follows: First two days for Burha family, next two days for Deka family, 3rd two days for Brahma family, 4th two days for Hota family, 5th two days for Bidhipathak family.

Pali of *Nittya Puja*

	2	2	2	2	2
	Buhra	Deka	Brahma	Hota	Bidhipathak
1st 10 days	Buhra	Deka	Buhra	Hota	Bidhipathak
2nd 10 days	Buhra	Deka	Deka	Hota	Bidhipathak
3rd 10 days	Buhra	Deka	(1 Hota+1 Bidhi)	Hota	Bidhipathak

5 days Panchaparba, 30-5 = 25 days

Sevaks and Their Duties

1. Athporia or Astho Prohari who are responsible for security and cleanliness inside the temple,
2. Bayan performs dance at the time of worship of the deity,
3. Bheru are the *Sankha badak* (conch players),
4. Bharali are the store keeper,

5. Bhandar kayastha prepares list of the items required for the worship of the deities,
6. Bolikatas are involved in sacrificing of the offered animals,
7. Bolidhara assists during sacrifice of the offered animal,
8. Duari are responsible for door keeping,
9. Dhulia are drum beaters,
10. Danda-Chatradhari holds danda and chatra,
11. Gayan sings song during worship of the deity,
12. Kahara-dhartekela is the bodyguard of Doloi,
13. Kaur khedia drives away birds/crows etc.
14. Kharidia are the wood suppliers,
15. Mudair are the treasurers,
16. Panieri is responsible for supplying of potable water and water for bathing of the deities,
17. Sitiniar cleans interior of the temple and Bhog ghar.

The above *sevakas/sevaits* enjoy hereditary rights to *seva-puja*.

Administration of the Temple: Development through Ages

Administration of the Kamakhya temple has been changed many times since Ahom rules till post-Independence.

From the reign of Gadadharsimha (1681-1698), all the power regarding temple was vested on the Daloi. The term Daloi has several meanings. It is derived from the Sanskrit word 'dal' meaning 'a collection of people'. The other meaning of the word 'Dal' is temple or a holy shrine and the word '*Daloi*' is derived from this to mean the chief of a Hindu temple in Kamrup. In Kamrup district all the civil and revenue matters of a temple were managed by the Daloi; he is the custodian of all the properties, movable and immovable and the receiver of all the donations from the devotees. During the Ahom rule, the Daloi was the chief of the temple and only people belong to Bardeori families were appointed to the office of the Daloi.

After the annexation of Assam by the British Government of India some changes were made as an experiment with regard to the temple. As a result, in 1834, the lands and fisheries known as Bhogdhani properties were settled in the names of the Dalois on behalf of the temples. With such vested power Daloi became a rich Zamindar and the honour of his office became so important and respectable that many distinguished families of Assam began to use the title of Bar Daloi (the chief of the Bardeoris). This was how Daloi continued his office in Kamrup till 1960. In 1961 the Assam Act IX, 1961 (the Assam State Acquisition of lands belonging to Religious or Charitable Institute of Public Nature Act, 1960) was enacted whereby all the lands of the temples were acquired and a fixed amount was sanctioned to each temples for their maintenance. The post of the Daloi was abolished and provisions for a managing committee for the maintenance and administration of the temples were made. In older days there were *Sastrakars* who were assigned to frame laws or code of conduct regarding the management of the temple.

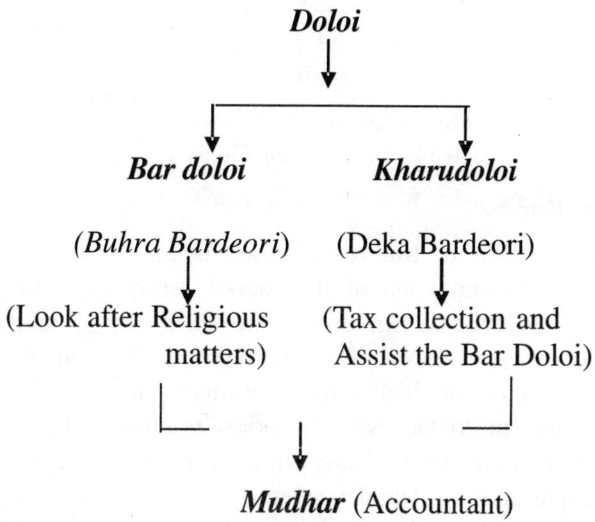

Now the Administration of the Temple is running by the Kamakhya Debutter Board which came into existence on 25th October, 1998. This Board is constituted of people who have been serving in the temple as a priest/*sebayat*. The chairman of the Board compulsorily hails from Bardeori group of Brahmins

(Burha). He is an elected member. He holds highest status among the members of the Board.

Structure of Debutter Board

Chairman and president [Bardeori/Barapujari (Burha)]

↓

Vice President

↓

Secretary [Barapujari]

↓

Adviser [Barapujari, Chandi Pathak]

↓

Members [*Nanan Pujari* and *Sevakas* like Bhandari, Duary, Atparia etc.]

The board employs people for different jobs like accountant, Store-in-charge, P.R.O., Incharge of Guest house, *Safaiwala* etc.

Observation

Nilachal hills of Kamrupa, Assam being abode of goddess Kamakhya, became one of the sacred centre for pilgrimage. Under the doctrine of Hinduism *tirtha yatra* or pilgrimage is an important aspect in respect of its rebirth theory. Through pilgrimage to sacred centres one can achieve ultimate salvation. Therefore people come in contact with the priest frequently. Priest offers worship on their behalf. Here priest is the bridge between the devotee and divinity. The dependency on priests for the religious service brings the devotees close to the priests. The priests on the other hand take care of the local hospitality of the devotees. This close interaction between them establishes a *jajmani* relation with the *sevayats*. Such relationship survived over centuries through generations. Most of the people come here to propitiate the deities or even for *darshan* in order to earn *punya* (virtue). In this process a large number of devotees have established *Jajmani* ties with the *sevayat* Brahmans. Besides earning *punya* (virtue), devotees also come for marriage and other ceremonies to be performed under the auspices of the temple. Socially unapproved marriages are often solemnised at the temple which gives sacred sanction and consequent approval in the society.

The most unique and interesting feature is the method employed by the priests to maintain *'Jatrik Khata'* which contains information about the family/lineage of a devotee over a few generations. The attachment of devotees to a particular clan of priests, over generations, who take care of all their needs during their visits to the temple, is another important aspect of this priest-devotee link up. Eventually, the method of recording information about the devotee has not been changed. The traditional customs and practices associated with the system are still in use. The detailed family history and genealogical data stored in the *khata* are of immense value to both the priests and devotees. This system helps the priests to derive economic benefits and provide the devotees guaranteed personalised services, support for worship and performance of rituals etc. In this unique priest-devotee relationship, the key factor is the *'Jatrik Khata'* which forms the primary reference point. The *'Jatrik Khata'* is also frequently used by the devotees, their families, courts and authorities to identify individual family trees, establish/confirm genealogical relationships, trace migration of the family and so on. The intricate and indexed records of data in the *"Jatrik Khata"* are also valuable from the archival point of view. It is thus felt that the tradition needs to be protected and preserved.

It is also a fact that the situation is changing fast in the recent days. Nowadays though the visitors are coming in larger numbers, but as their stay is of a short duration, the relationship is gradually becoming impersonal, transient and contractual and the scope of establishment of permanent bond is gradually becoming remote. As the numbers of temporary clients are fast increasing, it has also created a competition among the *sevayats*. Consequently, conflicts which was rarely seen in the past are not too uncommon now-a-days. The traditional *Jajman-Sevayat* relationship is gradually becoming feeble and less effective. The patronage and help received from the well to do *jajmans* are fast decreasing. It may be added here that the persons who are attracted by modern media of communication are mostly transitory visitors without having any *jajmani* relationship.

Previously the Brahmins used to write Banshabali (genealogical record) of the devotees on the khasi pat/Sanchi pat which has been replaced with paper. Now with the easy communication system and development of tourism the devotees do not stay in the Pandā's houses like olden days. Now the devotees prefer to stay in hotels/guest houses in Guwahati. It is expressed often that previously the devotees used to pay generously as *dakshina* to the priest/*savayats*. But now that bond is getting diluted.

However, the tradition is continuing. The huge storage of data about the pilgrims over centuries has immense importance in understanding the development of the sacred centres as well as the socio-religious psyche of Indian society as a whole. All such great centres of religious importance act as a melting pot for the diverse racial and cultural tradition in a pluralistic society like India.

Acknowledgement

We express our sincere gratitude to the Director, Anthropological Survey of India, for giving an opportunity to visit Kamakhya Temple, for the collection of data. We are also thankful to the Head of Office of Anthropological Survey of India, Eastern Regional Centre, Kolkata, for all kind of administrative and academic support. We owe greatly to the President, Secretary and all the members of the Debutter Board of Kamakhya Temple, for their kind cooperation during field work. Without their support this study would not have been possible. Special thanks to Sri Kamal Sharma Barapujari, Sri Pratap Chandra Sharma Barapujari, Sri Nagen Sharma Barapujari, Sri Biraj Sharma, Sri Sukhen Sharma, Sri Anup Sharma, for their kind cooperation.

Annexure 1

Kamakhya Temple Complex

Dasa-Mahavidya: Dasa-mahavidya, the ten deities are believed to be the various forms of Durga, the symbol of energy. The ten forms are:

1. Kali, dark in colour and fierce in character,
2. Tara, a benign form of Sakti,
3. Sodasi, when the goddess is of sixteen,
4. Bhuvanesvari,
5. Bhairavi,
6. Chinnamasta, who is headless holding her own severe head in one hand,
7. Dhumavati, who is a widow,
8. Bagala, who is the destroyer of enemies,
9. Matangi and
10. Kamala

Shiva Temples

1. Kauti Linga Temple
2. Amra Tokoreswar Temple
3. Kedareswar Temple
4. Kameswar Temple
5. Siddheswar Temple

Other Temples

1. Jai Durga Temple
2. Bana Durga Temple
3. Namath Kali Math
4. Hanuman Temple
5. Ganesh Temples
6. Pandunath Temple

7. Gadadhar Vishnu Temple
8. Shitala Temple

***Kundas* (Ponds)**

1. Saubhagya Kunda
2. Wrin Mochan Kunda
3. Amrit Kunda
4. Durga Kunda
5. Gaya Kunda
6. Varaha Kunda
7. Karso Pukhuri

Annexure 2

Sorosapachar

1. *Asan* (seat),
2. *Shagatam* (welcome),
3. *Padyam* (paduka),
4. *Arghyam* (kosha-dusi),
5. *Aasan anguri* (ring),
6. *Madhu Pakkya* (a mix of clarified butter, honey, curd and sugar),
7. *Puna asman,*
8. *Sringar* (articles for bath),
9. *Bastra* (cloth),
10. *Alankar* (ornaments),
11. *Dhup* (lamp),
12. *Avaran* (sindur/vermillion, sankha/conch shell, mirror, comb),
13. *Sajjya* (bed for rest, made of velvet and silver),
14. *Mishtannya* (sweets),
15. *Naivedya* (offerings of fruits, sweets and *bhog* etc.) and
16. *Sacrifice* (of pigeon, he goat, he buffaloes etc.).

Annexure 3

Festivals of Kamakhya Temple

Sl. No.	*Festivals*	*Months*
1.	Makar Sangkranti (Magh Bihu)/ Uttarayan Sangkranti	January
2.	Ratanti Kali Puja	January/February
3.	Saraswati Puja	January/February
4.	Shivarati	February/March
5.	Dol Yatra (Holi)	March
6.	Durga Dol and Shiva Dol	March/April
7.	Basanti Puja	March/April
8.	Madan Puja	March/April
9.	Chaitra Sankranti (Bohag Bihu)	April
10.	Gramya Devata Puja	May/June
11.	Ambubachi Mela	June
12.	Dakshinang Sankranti (Kali Puja)	July
13.	Manasa Puja (Debaddhani)	August
14.	Krishna Janmastami	August/September
15.	Durga Puja	October
16.	Lakhsmi Puja	October
17.	Kartik Sankranti (Kati Bihu)	October/November
18.	Shyama Puja (Dipawali)	November
19.	Dhanya Chedan	November/December
20.	Katyayani Brata, Sadhan Brata	November
21.	Pohan Biya/Hara Gauri Bibah	December/January

Bibliography

Adhikary, Gajendra (2001) A history of the Temple of Kamrup and their Management Chandra Prakash, Panbazar, Guwahati.

_______(2006) Religious Establishments of Assam, Studies in their Socio-Economic Background, Guwahati.

Allen, B.C. (1904) Assam District Gazetteers, Vol. IV, Kamrup, Pioneer Press.

Amanatullla, A A History of Coochbehar.

Barapujari, H.K.'The Management and Control of the Religious, Endowments in Assam (1825 – 58)', published in the journal of the University of Guwahati, Vol. XV No.1 Arts 1964, p. 35.

Barua, S.L. (1985) A Comprehensive History of Assam Delhi. Munshiram Manoharlal Publication.

Baruah, Padmanath (1906) Asamar Burungi, or the History of Assam, Tezpur Lila Agency.

Basu, N.N. (1986) The social History of Kamrupa, Vol. 2, 2nd Reprint New Delhi.

Bhuyan, Surjya Kumar (1931) A History of Assam, 1681-1826 A.D. 1st ed. Guwahati, Directorate of Historical and Antiquarian Studies of Assam.

Borooah Bahadur, (1900) Assam Burnji or the History of Assam including the Goonabhiram history of the Ancient kingdom of Kamrup from the Earliest time and containing a brief note of the caste Language, Religion, commerce Agriculture, Arts and Social customs of the people and the Internal Govt. of the Province. 4th ed. Calcutta. Monica Press.

_______Brahma – Baivartapuram, Sri Krasna Yanmakhanda, (39-40-57).

Barua, Rudreshwar and Rajendra Library, Kolkata Shaktipada Chakraborty

Barua, B.K. and H.V.S. (1965) The Temple and Legends of Assam, p. 29, Murthy, Bombay.

Bose, M. L. (2003) Social History of Assam, Concept Publishing Company, New Delhi.

Bose, M. L. (1985) Development in Administration in Assam, Concept Publishing Company, New Delhi.

Barua, K.L. (1945) Early History of Kamrupa, Guwahati.

Bucehanon – Hamilton, F Account of Assam, 1807-14, Calcutta.

Basu, N.K. (1965) Assam, in the Ahom Age, Calcutta.

Bose, M.L. (2003) Social History of Assam, Concept Publishing Co. New Delhi.

Barua, Rudreshwar Mahatirtha Kamakhya, Rajendra Library Kolkata-1 Shaktipada Chakraborty

Barapujari, Debsharma (1416) Kamakhya Tirtha Assam Book Depo, Panbazar, Dharanikanta Guwahati

Bardoloi, Dr Nirmal Prabha (1986) Debi Sahitya Prakash, Guwahati.

Barapujari, H.K. (ed) (1990) The Comprehensive History of Assam, Volume-I, Publication Board.

Chatterjee, Sarajitkumar (2010) North-East India: Dispersion and Discontent. Vol.1Abhijit Publication, Delhi.

Chatterjee, S.K. (1955) The place of Assam in the History and civilisation of India. Guwahati University of Guwahati.

Chodhury, P.C. 1966 (1959) The History of civilisation of the people of Assam To the Twelfth century A.D. Guwahati : Directorate of Historical and Antiquarian studies of Assam.

Chaudhury, Anima: Temples and shrines in and around Guwahati: A Sociological and Folkloristic Exploration.

Chakrabory, Abharani (2005) Punnya Tirtha Kamakhya, Sabita Prakash, Guwahati.

Debsharma Barapujari Kamakhya Tirtha, Kalibhavan, Kamakhya.

Dharanikantya (1416) Guwahati.

Deka, Pranb Jyoti (2004) Neelachala Kamakhya Her History and Tantra, Kanwachal Road, Guwahati, Assam.

Daloi Sharma, H. N. (1983) As a mat Sakti Sadhana Aru Sakta-Sahitya.

D.D. Kosambi (1970) The Culture and Civilisation of Ancient India in Historical Outline. p. 146. Vikas Publishing House Pvt. Ltd.

Ernest Mackay (1948) Early Indus Civilisation. p. 144, Luzac & Co. London.

Gait, E (1906) A History of Assam, Shillong, p. 121.

Hunter, W. W A Statistical Account of Assam, Vol. I and II, reprint.

Hazra, R.C. (1975) Studies in the Puranic Records on Hindu Rites and Customs, pp. 249-253. Motilal Banarsidrs.

Iswara Topa (1940) Our Cultural Heritage, Some of Essentials of Indian Civilisation. p. 41, Kitabistan: Allahabad.

Kakati, B.K. (1948) The mother Goddess Kamakhya Publication Board, Guwahati, Assam.

Kakati, B.K. (1978) The Mother Goddess Kamakhya. Guwahati: Lanyens Book Stall.

Karma Purana Part – 1, Chapter XII, 64/1, 64/2, 64/79.

Kosambi D.D. (1970) The Culture and Civilisation of Ancient India in Historical outline, p. 176, Vikash Publishing House, Delhi.

Mishra Bhivuti Bhusan A Historical Study of Religious Beliefs and practices of North India during the early medieval period.

Mishra, Kamal K (2005) Indigenous knowledge, Natural resource Manage mentand Development. The Konda Reddy Experience, Bhopal and New Delhi: IGRS, Pratibha Prakasan. The World Intellectual Property Organisation document. WIPO Pub 920. pdf, HYPERLINK "http://www.WIPO.Int/ebookshop".

Neog, M (ed) (1974) Prachya Sasanavli, Guwahati.

Neog, M (1969) Pabitra Assam, p. 302.

N.N. Bhattacharya (1975) Ancient Indian Rituals and their Social contents. pp. 75-78, Manohar Book Service, Delhi.

Nath R.M. (1936) Kalapahar and Kamakhya Temple' in *JARS*, Vol. IV, July, No. 2, pp. 42-46.

Saikia Yasmin (2005) Assam and India Fragmented Memories, cultural Identity and the Tai-Ahom struggle. Permanent Black, Delhi.

Sarma, Ganga (1978) Mother Goddess Kamrupa Kamakhya, published by Mritunjoy Sarma, Vishnu Prakashan, Kamakhya.

Sarma, P.C. (1988) Architecture of Assam, Delhi, p. 107.

Sastri, B.N., (1979-80) 'Destruction of the Kamakhya temple as referred in the Yogini Tantra', in *JARS*, Vol. XIV, pp. 6-7.

Sharma, D. (1981) Kamarupasasana Vali Guwahati: Publication Board Assam.

Sharma, Rajiv (2002) Mahamaya Sri Sri Kamakhya Devir Mahatya. The History and Heritage Research Centre of Sri Kamakhya, Kamakhya Debottar Board, Kamakhya Dham, Guwahati, Assam.

—— An Annual Shamanistic Dance (Deodhanae) at Kamakhya, Assam in the Journal of the University of Guwahati, Vol. XI, Science ed. M. Neog, 1960.

The Kalika Purana (1384) Navabharat Publishers, Calcutta.

Vasu N.N. (1922) Social History of Kamarupa, Calcutta.

Yogini Tantra ——In JARS, Vol. XIV, 1979-80, pp. 6-7. (1913) Webster's Dictionary.

Neog M. (2001) cited from Adhikary Gajendra: A history of temple of Kamrup and their Management, pp. 8-14, Chandra Prakash, Panbazar, Guwahati. (PS, Plate No. 3).

Kamakhya Temple, Assam.

Devotees at Kamakhya Temple, Assam.

Devotees Offering Puja at Kamakhya Temple, Assam.

Crowd of Devotees at Kamakhya Temple, Assam.

Preservation of *Banshabali* at Kamakhya Temple, Assam.

Banshabali.

Preservation of *Banshabali.*

Ancient *Banshabali* Records.

Ancient *Banshabali* Records at Kamakhya Temple.

Performing Lifecycle Ritual at Kamakhya Temple.

Recent *Banshabali* Records

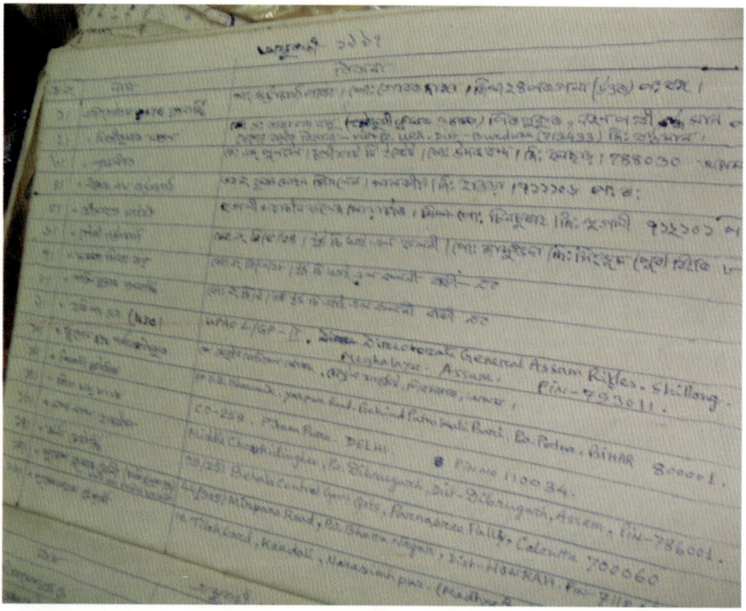

Plate 1.

Plate 2.

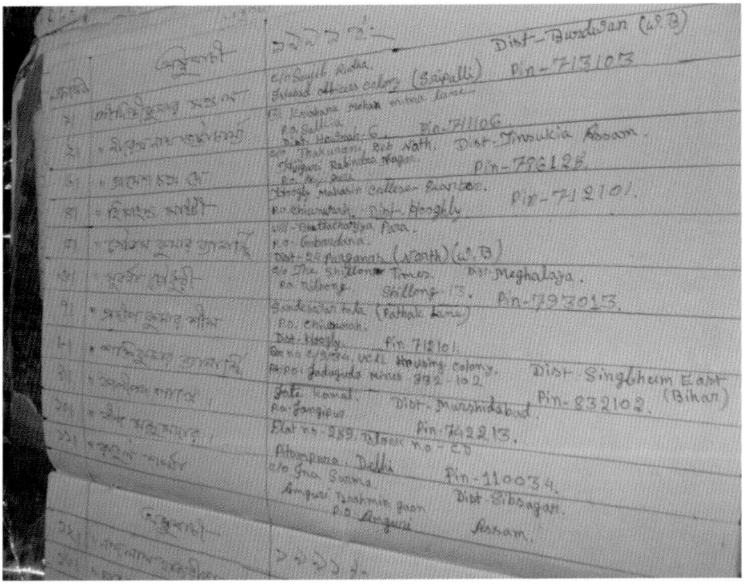

Plate 3.

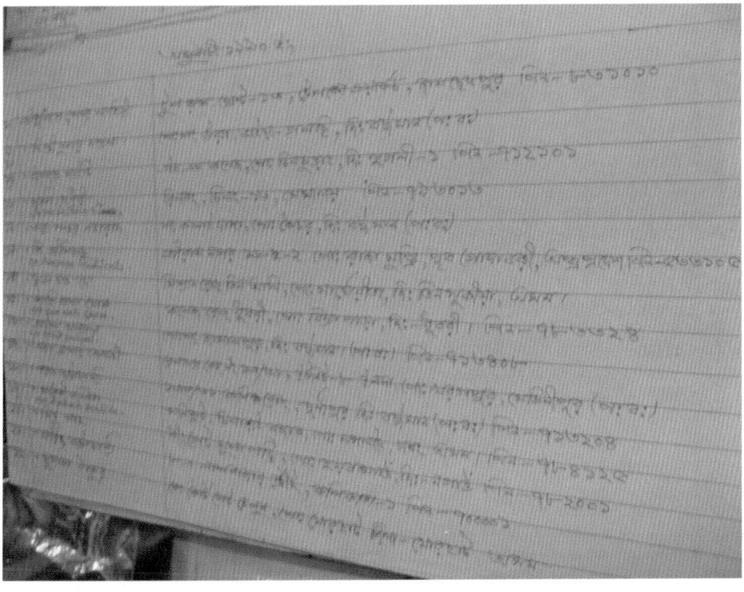

Plate 4.

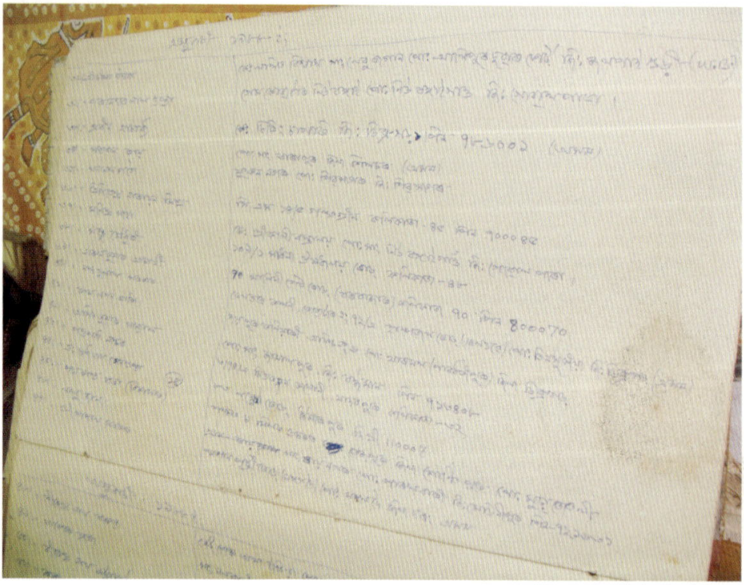

Plate 5.

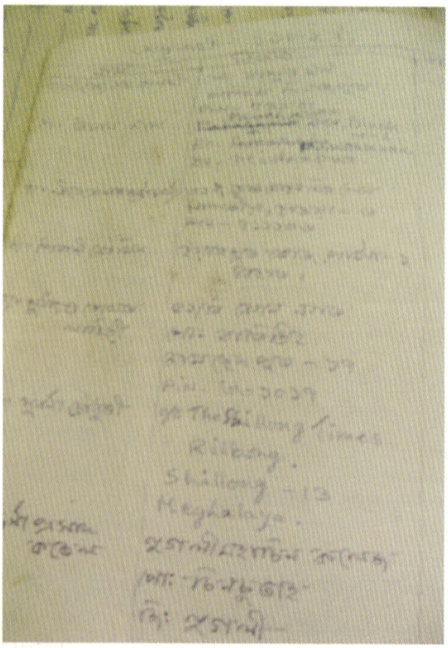

Plate 6.

Plate 7.

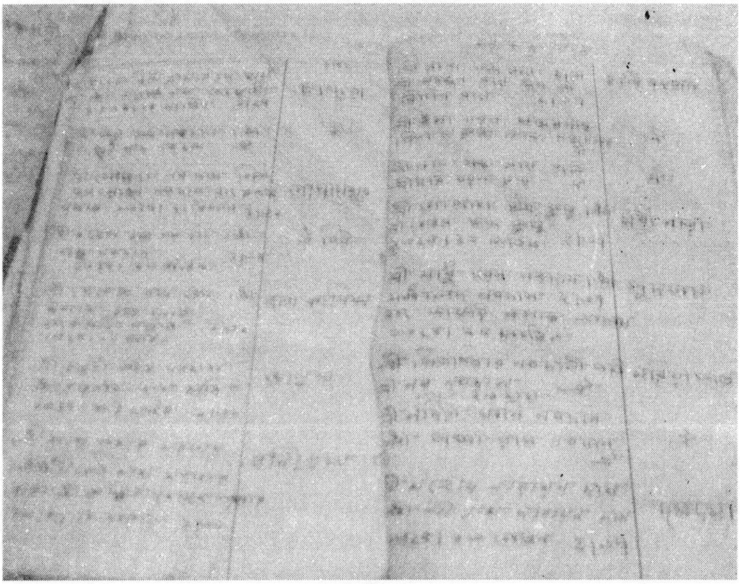

Plate 8.

Plate 9.

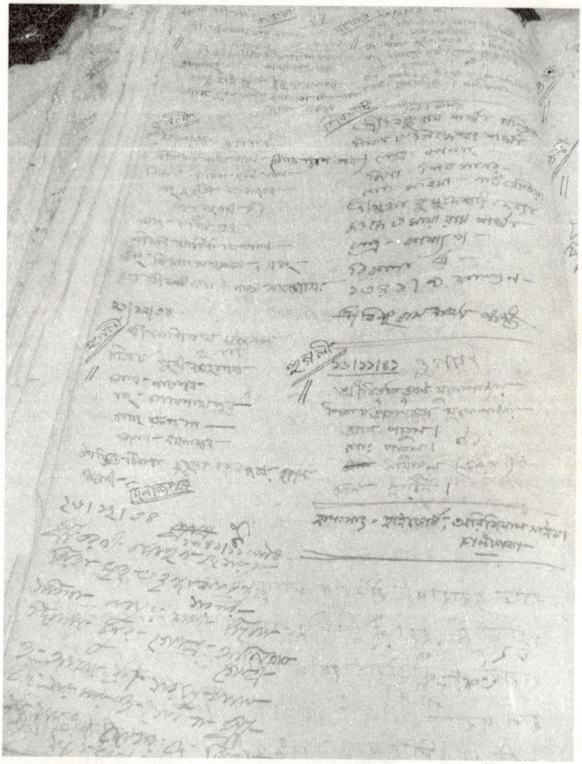

Plate 10.

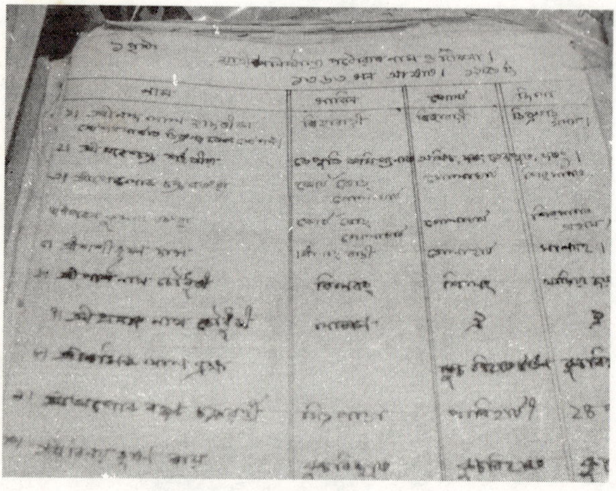

Plate 11.

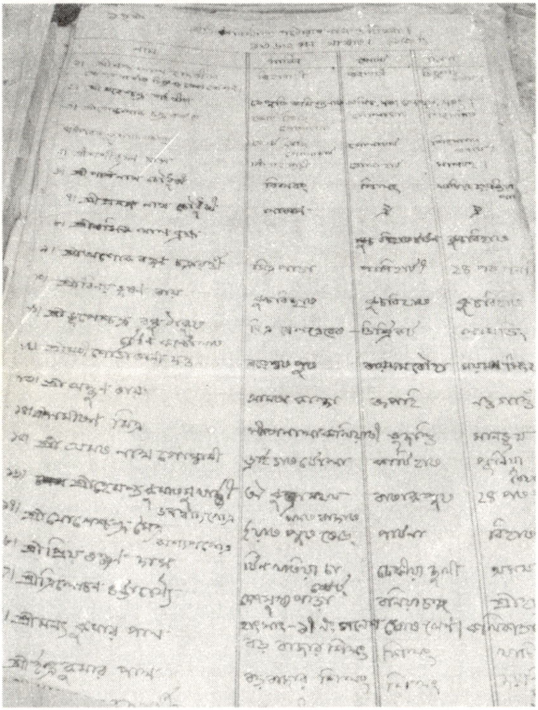

Plate 12.

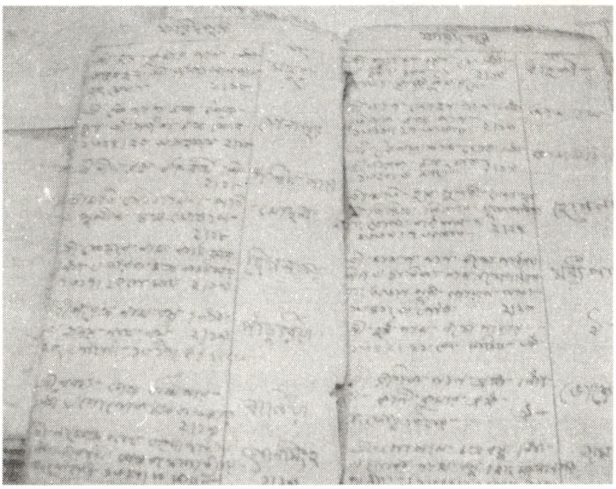

Plate 13.

4

Study of Rameswaram Temple: Religious Significance and Traditional Knowledge of Record Maintaining System

K.M. Sinha Roy

Introduction

Religion is a universal phenomenon in human society. It is professed in various forms in different societies. Religion can be described as a sum total of social values and unwritten customary order which influences the human beings consciously or unconsciously. People worship supernatural beings in the form of various God and Goddesses, sometimes morphic and sometimes amorphic, to gain spiritual power or mental satisfaction. In the Hindu pantheon there are innumerable number of Gods and Goddess, each having a place in Hindu mythology. Each god or goddess is believed to have specialised power that may affect some or other arena of human life and accordingly they are appeased through worship for the welfare at individual, family and community level.

The Hindu society is divided into a hierarchical system of Varna order, based on division of labour, where Brahmins occupy the highest position in social order followed by the Kshatriya, Vaishya, and Sudra respectively. In the Vedic rites a Brahman serves as priest and he mediates between the deities, the supernatural beings and the devotees. A devotee can not offer *puja* (worship) on his own, a priest's service is essential to offer worship to the deities. Therefore, the position of a Brahmin as priest is attached with superior social values in the society. It has also been depicted through history, literatures and epics that Brahmins held power and thereby occupied high positions in different governing bodies in different dynasties, like as advisor to the King, as Raj Jyotishi (Astrologer for the king), as Pandit (vernacular or Sanskrit scholar) or Raj *Purohit* (priest for the king), which proves the persistence of such tradition since ancient times. The priestly service by the Brahmins is still continuing in spite of transformation of society to the age of modernisation; they still serve as priests in temples, religious places, and in socio-religious rites and rituals.

In Hinduism pilgrimage is an important part of religious activities for the devotees and there are different pilgrimage centers for different sects. It is believed that pilgrimage to sacred centers not only brings mental satisfaction and welfare for the family but it also opens the passage towards heaven. While worshipping the deities in various sacred centre or temples a devotee requires priestly services and thereby comes in contact with the local temple priests. Under such circumstances there developed a kind of reciprocal relationship between the priest (Brahmin) and the devotee, that persists from generation to generation and such relationship also develops a socio-economic dependency between the Priest and the devotees.

In this context as discussed above, the Rameswaram Temple in Tamil Nadu occupies a significant position. The nexus of this temple is traced from the great epic of *Ramayana*. It is believed that at this place Lord Rama, worshipped Siva. The place is also called as holy Kashi and equated with the great sacred centre of Kashi (Benaras/Baranasi) in the State of Uttar Pradesh. It is believed that if one dies at Benaras (Kashi) his soul achieves *mukti*, ultimate salvation of soul, while in Rameswaram just on *darsana* (the holi sight) of the deity one achieves *mukti* and gets relieved from all kinds of sin. The place is also important as one of the twelve Jotirlinga sthalas, the great sacred centres under the doctrine of Saivism. The Jotirlingam of Rameswaram is called Ramalingam. Besides being a Saivait religious centre, Rameswaram is also an important pilgrimage centre for the Vaishnavites, the professors of Lord Vishnu. Under Vaisnavism there are four major sacred centres (*dham*) in India; they are Rameswaram, Badrinath, Kedarnath and Jagannath *Dham*. Rameswaram is revered as the *sayan kshetra*, the resting place of the Lord.

In Rameswaram, the people from different corners of the country come for pilgrimage and it has become an expression of unity between different religious sects. Spiritually it unites the Saivaites and Vaishnavites. There are four important temples of which Ramanatham (Rameswaram) is the Siva Temple and the other three are Vaishnav temples. The importance of Rameswaram Temple goes with the story that Lord Rama, who was the incarnation of Lord Vishnu, worshipped Lord Siva in the form of sivalingam here before starting his journey to Lanka, the kingdom of Ravana, the demon king, to rescue his wife Sita from the clutches of Ravana and therefore it is sacred to both Saivaites and Vaishnavites.

Historical Background

The empirical record reveals that, the area was exposed to diverse political interventions by different kingdoms from time to time. On the long journey of history, the area was ruled by the Marava, the Pandya, the Chola, the Ceylonese, the Muslim, the Portuguese, the Sethupatti, the British and finally the Government of India. Under diverse rulers different temples were built in different historical period. The great temple of Rameswaram was built in the seventeenth century on the site said to be sanctified by the footprint of lord Rama. Over such a long period of cultural transformation the temple of Rameswaram still maintains its age old tradition in pattern of worship and in other religious activities. In later period, some rulers brought Brahmin people from Maratha region (Maharashtra) for priestly services in the temple. Presently in the Rameswaram temple, two groups of Brahmin are involved in temple related activities: the local Tamil Brahmin and the immigrated Maharashtrian Brahmin. These Maharashtrian Brahmins were patronised by the kings largely to get them settle down in the land. It is said that they received land, gold, silver and other necessary items from the king to maintain their livelihood. Both the groups are still adhered to their traditional occupation.

The Rameswaram temple receives devotees from different parts of the country and also from Nepal and Sri Lanka. The Priest maintains the records of the devotees and note down the name of the devotee, the district and village where the devotee hailed from and other information. The records are maintained systematically for each devotee. The interaction between a particular family of devotee and a particular priest over a long period often resulted into a kind of relationship very similar to *jajmani* relation of traditional Indian society. Each priest works in his respective *Jajmani* area. The study probed into the process of this record maintaining system in the Rameswaram Temple and its adjacent temple; how the Brahmins maintain this age old tradition; their social status and economic condition as well as their religious commitment.

The historical background of the area unfolds wars and conflicts between the dynasties. The present Ramanathapuram district in the early days formed a part of the traditional Marava country. Numerous references of the Maravas are found in the Sangam works like Purananooru and Silappadhikaram. They refer them as inhabitants of Palai (desert, dry) land, one of the five types of land described in the Snagam literature. The recent theory connects them with the Malavar of ancient Kongu Nad; who are the races of Tamilnad in the first century A.D. Later they moved down to further south into the Pandya and the Chola countries. The present Ramanathapuram district was an integral part of the Pandya Kingdom and with the decline of power of the Pandyas it began to evoke itself into a separate entry.

Of the Pandyas, Maravarma Thirupuvana Chakravarthi Parakrama Pandya (1060-61) was contemporary of Kulotunga Chola I. In 1170, the Pandyas protracted internal warfare which arose on account of a disputed succession to the throne. Parakramabhahu, the ruler of Ceylon, played an important role in this war. Finally Kulasekara overpowered Parakrama Pandya, captured him with his family and put all of them to death. Later on a powerful force was sent under the famous general Lankapura Dandanatha. Lakapura successfully captured Rameswaram. Finally the whole of Marava country from Rameswaram to Tirupattur came under the sway of Lankapuram. The Mahayamsa, the Sinhalese epic described this invasion by Lankapura. The Ceylonese general immortalised his name by restoring peace through repairing of temples, tanks and construction of roads. The Ceylonese occupation and the Ceylonese general are remembered in the local oral tradition even to-day. It is interesting to note the local oral tradition about a Kandyan Monarch who built the sanctum-sanctorum of Rameswaram temple. This is evidenced by certain inscription in the sanctum itself. This ruler of Ceylon brought all the stone required for the building from Ceylon. The ships carrying the heavy stone landed at Talabilla and from there the stones were carried to the site of construction, since in the island of Rameswaram suitable stone were not available. It is said that the unused stones are still lying in the harbour at Pulliyadisalai.

After Maravarma Kulasekara's death, the Pandya kingdom was plunged into a fratricidal war which ultimately warranted the ruin of the kingdom. The Muslim force then marched across the Marava country, leaving desolation in its wake and arrived at Rameswaram. From the evidences available, it is surmised that he founded either at Rameswaram or on the mainland, a mosque which he named after his master Ala-ud-din Khilji. It is recorded that, this reigns ruled three Sultans successively namely Nadil shah, Fakir-ud-din Mubarak- Shah and Ala-ud-din Sikandar Shah till 1378 and the whole period was apparently uneventful.

The Marava country, with the fall of the Madurai sultanate passed under the Vijayanagar Empire. This fact is amply borne out by the Mrtynjaya manuscripts which say "the extent of the country acquired was from Uttatur (Urratur) and Valikondapuram on the north, even to Kanyakumari (Cape Comorin) on the south; to Covambutur (Coimbatore), Irodu (Erode), Tarapuram (Dharapuram) and Mela Mali (Mela Malai), Western Ghats on the west and Ramisseram on the east (Rameswaram)". Nelson and Rangachari are of the view that Viswanatha and his able minister Dalavoy ariyanthar ruled Marava country through two commissioners. But this administrative experiment soon failed. It was Muthu Krishnappa Nayakka (1601-1609) who effected the settlement of the Marava country.

In the middle of the 16th century the Portuguese had established them in Tuticorin, Vaipar and Punnaikayal. Francis Xavier landed in Tirunelveli coast in 1542 and carried on a hectic campaign. Meanwhile the Portuguese, with the co-operation of Paravas, who converted to Christianity, established Portuguese overseas province. They took over the civil and criminal administration of the fishery coast without getting prior sanction from any native potentate. Francis Xavier spoke of Paravas as "subjects of His Portuguese Majesty".

Finally the Nayakka decided to establish a strong power near the Portuguese establishments. The second factor, though economic, was also equally important. The Portuguese began to be benefitted by all the dues and revenues of the coastal area. More than anything else the revenue from the pearl fisheries went a long way in enriching their treasury. They thought that a strong power in the neighbourhood of the Portuguese territory would be a safeguard against their further extension. Finally the Viswanatha's administration failed to control the local problems. As a result, of the prevailing confusion the route to Rameswaram became unsafe due to their being infested with a number of way layers. The pilgrims constantly petitioned to the ruler, the Nayak, to make the road safe for travellers.

Later on, Muthukrishnappa Nayakka was the first king who arranged armed escorts to the pilgrims. The king was pleased with the Sethupathi and he appointed Sadaika Deva as the chief of the Poligars and the viceroy of Marava country by sprinkling the water of Ganges on his head and gave him the insignia of dignity. The Sethupathi started ruling the Marava country with the relegated authority. Sadaika Deva (1605-1621) had been a successful ruler and did much towards the peace and progress of the Marava country. An inscription at Rameswaram records his gifts to the temple; this area was granted with five villages in 1607 and another grant of land to the temple. He also made grants to the temple at Tiruvadanai. He is said to have bestowed proper attention to the management of religious and charitable institution of the country. The son of Sadaika Deva made additional endowments to the Tiruvadanai temple and extended the temple at Rameswaram.

The Sethupathi kingdom gradually declined and finally Ragunathan, the Nayak, introduced Telugu language in the area. During the time, Ragunathan introduced the Navarathiri, nine night's festival in this part of South India. This festival was celebrated with great pomp and splendor in Madurai by the Nayak. The festival is meant to worship goddess Durga. Even today the festival is celebrated at Ramanathapuram and at Rameswaram temple in the same way as introduced by Ragunatha Sethupathi. Ragunatha built a village at Rameswaram which was so located as to be accessible through the bridge built by Ramappaiya. From then on, he spent most of his days at Rameswaram. He immortalised his name in the annals of Rameswaram by performing the "Hiranyagarbha" sacrifice and thus owns the tittle Hiranya-garbhayaj which all the subsequent Sethupathi assumed. For the support of several Brahmin families he granted fifty villages. He also made grants to the Tiruvaduturai Mutt in the Thanjavur district. He built the Vanasankari Amman temple at Ramanathapuram.

Later on, for a very short term Rustom Khan estsblished a Muslim dynasty in Tiruchirapalli. During his time De Britto of the

Madura Mission worked for the spread of Christianity in India and earned great reputation.

Vijaya Sethupathi (1710-1725) was able to introduce some reforms. He was pious and devout. He granted several Dharmasanams (grants) to the Brahmins. He performed 'Hiranyagarbha Yagam' at Ramanathapuram and endowed the Kothanda Rameswaram temple of the same place. His special devotion to the Rameswaram temple got expressed through his munificent grants. He made important additions to the great temple. He used to offer worship daily in the evening in the temple. He geared up the administration and carefully attended to the care and conveyance of the pilgrims to Rameswaram. During the time, Rameswaram to Dhanushkodi march across to connected road.

After death of Sethupathi the kingdom collapsed. Later on Kattaya Thevar started his dynasty. He was also liberal in his religious and charitable endowments. About twenty villages were granted to the Brahmins as Dharmasams. Two of his leading civil servants, Pradanis as they were called Ramalinga Pillai and Vairavan Servai, who were in charge of the revenue administration of the country built temples respectively at Kulavayal and Peruvayal and got them endowed by the Sethupathi. In 1752, captain Cope had taken possession of a part of Madurai country on behalf of the Raja of Mysore. By this time, the Dutch were trying to secure a foot hold in the country. In 1759, Sethupathi granted the required permission by entering into a treaty with them. In the seventeenth century Dalavai Sethupathi built a part of east main Gopuram (tower). In the eighteenth century Ravi Vijaya Reghunatha Sethupathi built Palliyarai-Sayanagraha and the mandapam in front of the Amman Sannithy.

In the latter part of the eighteenth century the outer *Prakaram* was built by Muthuramalinga Sethupathi. The east Gopuram consisting of nine floors was constructed by the family of Devakottai, generally called Zamindar Veedu between 1897 and 1904. Between 1907 and 1925 they renovated the sanctum sanctorum and the innermost *Prakaram* was rebuilt with black granite. They were responsible for the performance of Kumbabhishkam in 1947. Now the temple complex is protected by strong and tall compound walls. The length of the wall in between East to West is 865 feet and between north and south is 657 feet. The temple has two great Gopuram with Kalasams at top on east and west entrances.

Rameswaram Island

The Rameswaram Island is the largest of the islets. The island forms part of the Adam's Bridge, extending east and west between Ceylon and the south-eastern coast of the peninsula at the entrance of the Palk Strait and forming the northern boundary of the Gulf of Manar. The consequent erosion is pretty heavy and the Railway track between the Dhanushkodi Pier and the Rameswaram road is now in very bad condition. Dhanushkodi is the worst sufferer due to erosion and a large part of the village site with numerous buildings is now under the sea swallowed by erosion. The western end of the Rameswaram Island has an extensive sand bank, known as Horse shoe Bank. Pearl and chunk fisheries and fishing are carried on, on an extensive scale on the coasts.

Rameswaram Island is divided into two survey villages, Pamban and Rameswaram. The latter includes the revenue village of Dhanuskodi. Interestingly, in agricultural practices in this island no plough is used for cultivating the land. The belief behind such practice is that the land where Lord Rama walked once should not be ploughed, i.e., should be restrained to make furrow in the land. Cultivation is done only by means of hoe. The major area is covered by tamarind and Odai trees. The islanders import their food grains from the mainland. Rameswaram town, Kothandaramaswami temple, Dhanushkodi, Mukundaroyar Chatram, Kundudugal temple, Pamban and Tangach-chimadam are the important places on the coast-line of the island. At present, one can reach Dhanushkodi on foot along the seashore or by Taxi and Jeeps or by boats. The Rameswaram Island is found in the shape of a shell (Chunk), supposed to be held by Lord Vishnu in his hand. Rameswaram is situated at a point where Bay of Bengal joins with Indian Ocean and in the popular belief Indian Ocean is identified as male, Rathnakaram and Bay of Bengal as female, namely Mahodhathi. The place plays a vital role in the Hindu religion. People come for ancestor worship and holy bath. The temple of Ramanatha is the most important place in the island.

The name Rameswaram is derived from Lord Rama. In Sanskrit language Rameswaram is called 'Devanagara' meaning the city of God (Deva=god; nagara=city). It is believed that Rameswaram was originally founded by Lord Rama after invasion to Lanka, identified with present day Ceylon. After killing Ravana, Rama sojourned at Gandha Mandhanam in the island of Rameswaram with Sita. The *Rishis* (Sages) advised Rama to establish a *Linga* (the phallic, symbolically Lord Siva) and worship it so as to purge himself of the sin of *Brahmahatya* (Brahminicide) committed by slaying Ravana, who was the son of a Brahmin by *Rakshasa* (demon) woman.

The Temple of Rameswaram is believed to be as old as of *Ramayana*, the great epic on the life of Lord Rama. It is said that the temple was initially of a thatched shed looked after by a hermit. The present structure was built up over centuries. However, the credit goes to the Sethupathis of Ramnad. The existing records show that in twelfth century, Parakrama Bahu, the king of Ceylon constructed the Sanctum Sanctorum around the Moolalinga (Sri Ramanathaswamy), Sri Viswanath and the Ambal shrine. In fifteenth century, Udayan Sethupathi of Ramnad and a Vaisya of Nagoor (near Nagapattinam) built the western stone of the compound wall which is about 78 feet high. A wealthy devotee from Madurai was responsible for constructing the Ambal Prakaram and some other renovation work. In the sixteenth century, Tirumalai Sethupathi built a portion of the southern second corridor. His statue and that of his son Ragunatha Sethupathi are found by the side of the southern entrance to the Ambal temple. They are honoured with flowers on every Friday. Later in the same century Chinna Udayan Sethupathi katta Thevar who was a feudatory under Viswanatha Naicker of Madurai made some additions including the Nandi Mandapam. In the seventeenth century Dalavai Sethupathi built a portion of the main eastern Gopuram. In early eighteenth century Ravi Vijaya Regunatha Sethupathi built the Palliyarai (Sayanagriha) and the Mandapam in front of the Ambal temple. Later in the same century, the World famous Third Corridor was constructed by Muthuramalinga Sethupathi.

Religious Significance

In Hindu philosophy 'mukti' or 'moksha', i.e., ultimate salvation of soul is most important and all religious behaviour and spiritualism are spearheaded towards the goal of achieving salvation. Pilgrimage to the Sacred Shrines and *Darshana*, the holy sight of the Lord, is one of the ways for such attainment. Pilgrimage helps a devotee to get blessings of God in order to live on earth in peace and after death to reach heaven. Therefore, pilgrimage or 'Sthala Yatra' is an essential part of one's earthily life. The holy rivers irrigate the fields, and also discipline the life of the people to receive heavenly and earthly joys. The roaring deep seas and their firmaments have been considered to be holy and they are still worshipped. The Ganges of Banaras and the Sethu of Rameswaram are such holy places.

Pilgrimage should start from Kashi (Banaras) and has to be completed in the Agni Theertham of Rameswaram. The antiquity, the familiarity and the popularity of this temple is equated with the great epic of '*Ramayana*'. The temple is sung in praise by Thiru Gnanasambandar, Thirunavukkarasar, Arunagirinadhar and Thayummanavar, the four great Tamil Saints. Rameswaram is revered for 'Moorthy, Theertha and Sthala'. There are a number of theertha each of which has its own importance in religious performances. The Mahalakshmi theertha or Lakshmi theertha is located south of the Sethupathy Mandapam and this is the first theertha inside the temple. Devotees who take a holy dip will enjoy all health and wealth. Gayathri, Savithri and Saraswathy theerthas are located north to the entrance of the third corridor of the Ramanathaswamy temple and east to the Natarajar shrine.

Dipping in these theerthas and worshipping the deities will bless the devotees to get rid of sins.

The story goes as follows:

Brahma, the God of creation once created a beautiful woman called Vakku. After creating her, *Brahma* got infatuated with her because of her beauty. He wanted to take her to bed. But she did not yield to his lustful intentions and ran away stating that as he created her he was her father. Brahma chased her. She took the form of various creatures to save herself from the lust of the Creator but Brahma kept on chasing her. Then Lord Siva appeared to save Vakku in the form of a hunter and threw an arrow which killed Brahma.

When the death news of Brahma reached his wives Gayathri and Saraswathy, they wanted to bring their husband back to life. They started doing penance and worshipping Siva. They created ponds in their names and offered prayers. They sustained themselves on food devoid of salt, once in a day. They continued to act like this for a long period in the Gandamadana mountain range.

Taking pity on the women doing penance, Lord Siva descended with his entourage of other *Devas*, *Rishis*, *Vasus*, heaven-livers, and Sivaganas and appeared before the wives of Brahma. They fell before Siva, chanted his holy name and worshiped him. Siva agreed to fulfill their wish. Gayathri and Saraswathy prayed for the life of their husband. Siva conceded the request of Gayathri and Saraswathy and brought Brahma back to life again. On getting back his life, Brahma prostrated before Siva and begged him to forgive his misdeed. Lord Parameswara was pleased and declared to Gayathri and Saraswathy that the ponds created by them at Gandamadana would go by their names. Woman dipping in the theertha and offering prayers would live as prosperous wife for a long time. Men who worship after bathing in the theerthas would also live prosperous life. They would have their sins washed away and reach heaven.

Chakra Theertham is located north of the madapalli, the second corridor and to the east of the holy temple. As it was created by *Rishi* Akirputhra, this theertha is also called *Rishi* theertha. The story is all about the fight between the *Devas*, the gods and the *Rakshasas*, the demons. The *Devas* were asked by the Creator to approach the Rishi (saint) of *sastras* and *astasiddhis* by name Akirputra who had obtained a *chakra* from Sudarsana perumal for protection against the attack of *Rakshas*. The *rishi* created a pond in the Gandamadana Mountain and performed the Maheswaram *yagna* peacefully with the help of the *chakra*. The *Devas* did their *yagna* at the same place peacefully. *Sethu Madha Theertham* is situated at the third corridor inside the temple. It is believed that, a dip in this Theertham brings blessings of goddess Lakshmi for the devotee. There are a number of such Theerthas and each of which is a holy place associated with some or other myth and legends like Kodi Theertham, Sarva Theertham, Chandra Theertham and so on.

Worship

In the district of Rammanathapuram, the major population belongs to Hindu religious faith followed by Islam and Christianity. Under the Hindu doctrine Saivism has a long history in the Marava country. During the period of the Pallavas, Saivism began to have deep roots in the Marava soil as evidenced by numerous Saivite temples of that age. A number of the Thevaram hymns have been sung in praise of the deities in some of these temples. The shrines of Thiruvadanai, Rameswaram and Kalaiyarkoil (Kannappar) are among those celebrated in the Thevaram hymns. The temple at Tiruvattarakosamangai is celebrated in the hymns of Saint Manickavasagar. The Saivite Nayanmar, Jlayangudi Maranayanar was a native of Ilayangudi which is in the heart of the Marava country. The Saivites worship Karuppannasamy and Bhadrakali, Maduraiveeran with offering of flesh and fruit. They have Saivite sectarian marks on their forehead.

Vaishnavism was also flourished eminently in the Marava country and Vaishnavite temples were patronised greatly by the ruling kings. Three such temples are Tirumayam, Tirukkoshtiyur and Tirupullani, which even today attract thousands of pious devotees all through the year. Besides, Mariamman, the mother goddess is propitiated extensively in the area. She is held in great veneration and is revered as 'Amma' (mother) or Mahamai (a corruption of the word Mahamayi). It is believed that her wrath would result in the spread of epidemics. And vows are often taken in the name of this goddess.

In the Rameswaram temple, religious activities are performed by both the priest groups. Rituals are elaborate and continue for the whole day. The major rituals observed are Thiruvananthal puja, Vila puja, Kalasanthi Puja, Uchikala puja, Sayaratcha puja, Arthajama puja, Palliarai Puja. The daily routine worship ends with Kal Vairabi puja. Beside regular *pujas* at scheduled times, *pujas* are also performed by the priests on behalf of each and every pilgrim as and when the devotee comes with his/her ticket obtained from the Devasthanam office. Pilgrims who wish to offer cash, gold or silver ornaments or other valuable articles should produce them before the temple Peishkar who will arrange to get them placed at the feet of the Lord or Devi as the case may be and get them entered in the temple account and issue proper receipts. Devotees who desire to endow lands or other immovable property should contact the treasurer or Executive Officer of the temple and arrange to have the prescribed Deeds executed with the approval of the Board of Trustees and Legal Officers. In Rameswaram a number of religious festivals are observed as part of the temple activities. The major festivals include Mahasivarathri, Vasantotsavam, and Ramalinga Prathishta.

Genealogical Record Maintaining System

Since long the devotees used to come to Rameswaram temple for offering worship and thereby achieving virtues and self purification. It is already mentioned that the devotees come not only from different corner of the country but also from the neighbouring countries like Sri Lanka and Nepal. The Devotees come mainly to offer Ganga water, the holy water to the Siva

Linga and to perform ancestor worship at Dhanuskutty. The local people come to the temple for ancestor worship as well as for performing marriage and birth rituals. The ceremonial observation of the first rice feeding to the baby is also observed in the temple by the local inhabitants. It is a part of the temple activities to record the name and other information about all the devotees and such records are maintained by the Priests. Other information includes the names of the village, district and the state which he or she belongs to. The Priest maintains a family register for each devotee and updates the family tree as and when anyone from the descending generation of that family comes on pilgrimage. A visiting family member is required to personally sign in the register, furnished by one's family priest after updating it for future family visitors and generations to see and to authenticate the updated entries.

In the Rameswaram temple the Maharastrian Brahmins mainly maintain the records. The local Devotees do not get their names entered into the record book. Today, these records play an important role in settling down legal cases regarding inheritance or property disputes, as these records are held sacrosanct both by the pilgrims and the priests, and in many places these records trace family history, for over twenty ascending generations, stretching across many centuries.

In Hindu Religion there are three ways of worshipping: Moorthy, Theertham and Sthalam. Rameswaram is distinguished as containing all these three characters. The temple as situated on the shore of sea is considered a holy Sthala, the sacred place. Of all the famous pilgrim centers in India Rameswaram is one of the most ancient holy places. It is said that the Sivalingam at Rameswaram had been installed by Sita Devi, the consort of Lord Rama. In worshipping the God a devotee depends on the priest (Brahmin) who performs the worship for the welfare of the Devotees. Through such interaction the priest and the devotees maintain a reciprocal relationship over generations. Such relationship is called *Jajmani*. The records are maintained so systematically that any time any record can be traced out. The system involves traditional knowledge.

It has already been stated that in Rameswaram temple, two groups of priests are involved in the temple activities; one, the local Brahmins and the other, the Maharastrian Brahmins. In Rameswaram the genealogical records are maintained by the Maharashtrian Brahmins only. Earlier there were fourteen such families who used to maintain the records. Presently only three families are maintaining the genealogical records. It is observed that under this record maintaining system the *Jajmans* mainly belong to the states of Maharashtra, Uttar Pradesh, Bihar, Madhya Pradesh, Haryana and to the neighbouring country of Nepal. People from Tamil Nadu, Andhra Pradesh and Kerala frequently visit the temple on different occasion but they never entered into this system.

As soon as a devotee arrives he/she makes a contact with the Priest for offering worship. The priests maintain records for their respective *Jajmans*. The devotees mainly come for ancestral worship. They approach their respective priest and perform worship. Accordingly, the priest makes an entry of their names along with the states, districts, villages they belong to, their caste, *gotra* and surname in a register called *boi*. *Boi* is the entry book. The priest finally transfers the records to a *khata*, the final register. In *khata*, the records are maintained in alphabetical order, first comes name of the state, then district, village, police station, caste, gotra, surname, present address (*hut mukam*) and finally the devotee is to sign to make the records authentic. Generally the records are maintained on paper. Ink is used for writing. The size of the register is about one meter in length and six inches in breadth. The khata is folded with red cloth and is preserved in wooden storing unit. Such records are useful to Court case mainly in cases related to land dispute. It is also observed that sometimes people collect the records for making family history.

The process of record maintaining system plays an important role in the field of religion, property dispute, and in drawing the genealogical chart of a particular family for the future generation. Apart, this traditional knowledge system helps in recovering the old records. In this system *Gomasta* and *Munibji* play a vital role on behalf of the Priest. *Munibji* maintains records in proper way in the two registers. The *Gomasta* assists the devotees in many ways; he brings them from Railway station, guides them up to the temple for worship, arrange their accommodation, food and medical facilities, and even go to the house of the devotees if required.

Genealogical Record Maintaining System

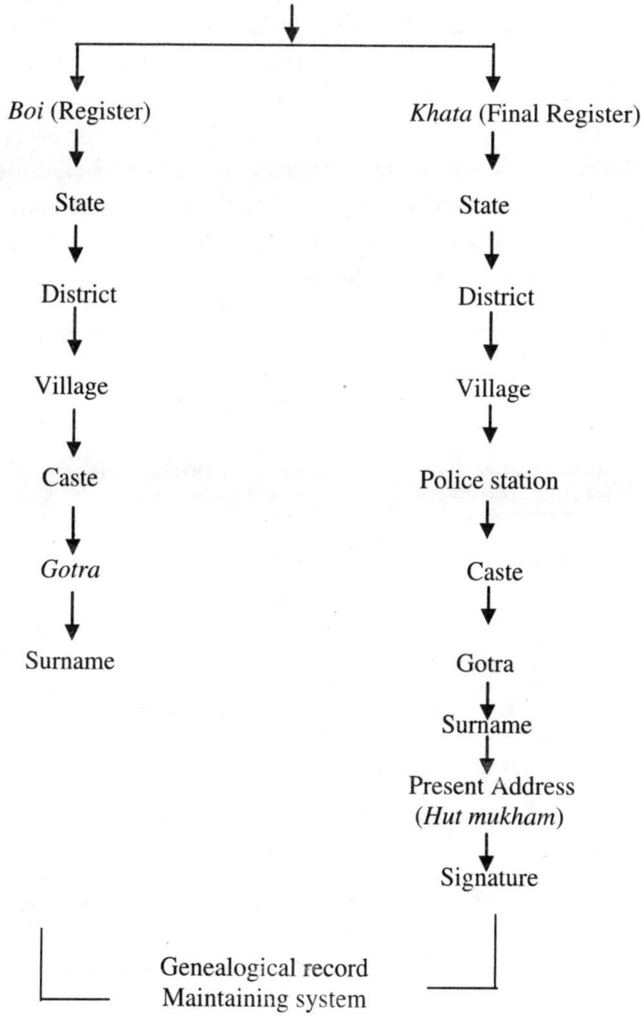

It has already been mentioned that in the Rameswaram temple, two types of priests are engaged in the religious activities: the Tamil Brahmin and the Maharashtrian Brahmin. There are further subdivisions in each of these categories. The Tamil Brahmins are divided into two categories: the Saivati Brahmin and the Vaisnavi or Vaisnavati Brahmin. The other group of Brahmins. i.e.. the Maharashtrian Brahmins is locally known as *Pujari*. According to one oral tradition, during the reign of Joy Raj Shel, the King of Aria Maharastra along with a group of Brahmins came to the area and he acquired the right to 'Shasankal' of the region and according to Aria Maharashtra *Banshabali* the priest acquired the right over temple worship, its gold, land, cows, forest and other properties for survival. Since then, the Maharastra Brahmins gradually settled down in the area and associated to Rameswaram temple and adjacent temples as priest and in due course taken up the activities as chief priest.

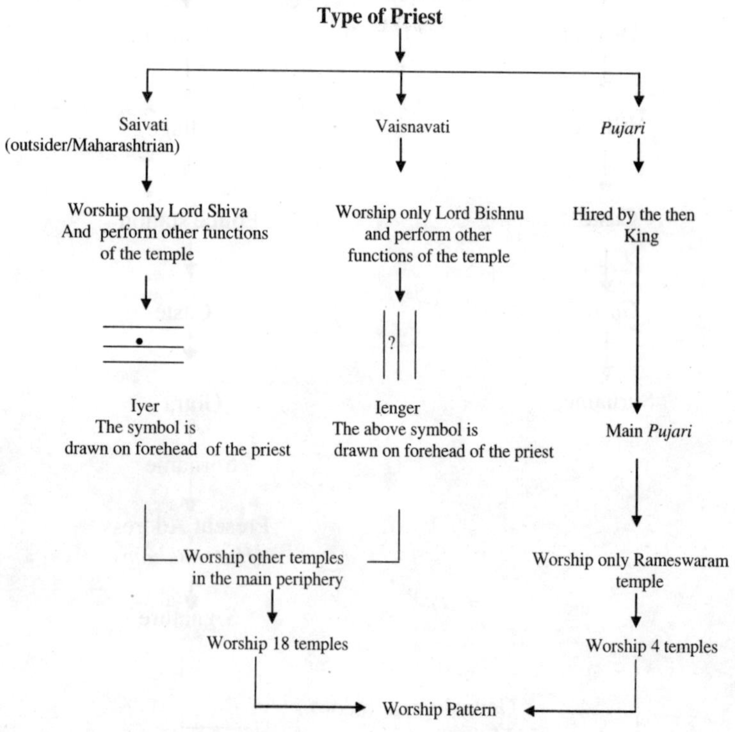

In Rameswaram temple there are altogether twenty two Gods and Goddess worshiped daily. The Saivati Brahmins are engaged in the worship of Lord Siva. The Vaisnavati priest performs worship in both inside and out side of the temple. The duties of various categories of priests are fixed since the early days of king's ruling and are continuing over generation to generation. Besides, the local priests offer their specialised services on different occasion of life cycle rituals to the people in an around the temple. The local people mainly come for *adi shynna* (the holy dip in the month of Shrabna Amabshya) and for *tai* (the holy dip in Pausha Amabshya). Besides, people also come for worship on the occasion of marriage, birth, rice giving ceremony, etc., and also in occurrence of death. A huge number of people come from the state of Kerala for observing the ancestral worship and to perform the rites of first rice giving ceremony to the child. The *Pujari* group of priests performs worship at four temples; it is also noticed that, the Pujari group of priests occupied higher social status among the Brahmins. The worship rites and rules and regulations of the temple remained unchanged since the olden days of king's ruling.

Taboos

The Priest observes some taboos on certain occasions. In occurrence of birth and death in family they observe pollution for a certain period (it is eleven days in case of birth and 13 days in case of death) and during this period the priest cannot join to temple activities. Even he is forbidden from entering into the temple premises. After the pollution period the family observes purification rites with the help of Kulo Guru, the family priest and thereafter the priest resumes his duties at the temple. The birth pollution is known as Shirapu-titetu and the death pollution as Erappu- titetu.

During the period of menstruation of any of female members in the family the priest is allowed to perform the worship but that in case of his wife he is tabooed to touch his menstruating wife and to cohabit with her. The practice is locally known as *Mada Bidai*.

In the temple the Shankaracharchya, King of Nepal is allowed to visit the temple any time; in case of other prominent guests or VIPs prior information is to be given to the temple administration and the administration arranges their visit. Around temple there developed numerous Maths and religious institutions. These Mathas and Institutions assist the devotees in various ways like providing food and medical facilities. The local administration as well as the temple administration provides budgets to these organisations to run welfare activities for the devotees.

Division of Labour inside the Temple

In Rameswaram temple duties of the priests and other temple servitors are fixed. Some of them are directly involved in the temple activities like priests, assistant of the priest, musical performers, Mahut (elephant driver), cook, etc., and others are indirectly associated with the temple like flower suppliers, milk man and suppliers of other items related to temple worship. Everyone is performing his duties as allotted by the kings to their forefather in ancient times. The responsibilities are being carried out over generations under the supervision of the administrative body of the temple. Nowadays sometimes the temple administrative body selects the candidates for some or other duties through interviews. The Priest and other servitors of the temple get salary for their service.

Main *Pujari* and their Division of Work

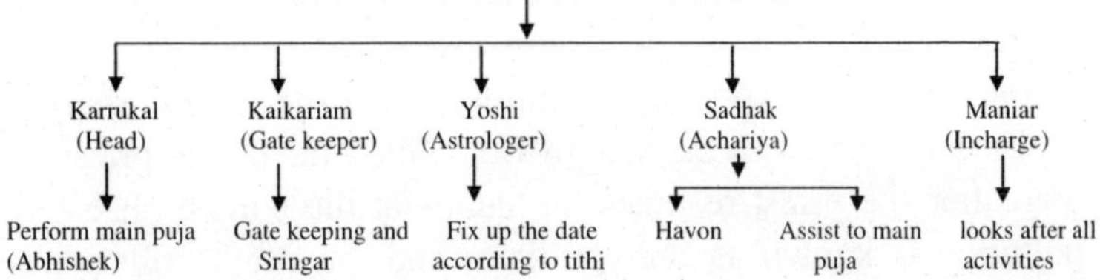

The main priest (pujari) of the temple is locally known as Kurrukal. He belongs to Maharashtrian group of Brahmin. He performs worship in the four temples: the temples of Lord Siva, goddess Parvati, Lord Bishanathan and goddess Bisha Laxmi. These four temples earn special attention of the devotees. The deities are offered *puja* for six times a day. Worship is performed by the main *pujari*. Til (sesame) oil, flower, Tamarind flower, rice mixture, Banana, milk, ghee (clarified butter), sugar and Ganga water are the essential holy ingredients for worship. Another essential item is *Panchamrita* prepared with banana, milk, ghee, sugar and honey. As soon as *puja* is over *Panchamrita* is distributed among the devotees; it is revered as blessings of the deity. The post of the priest is hereditary and succession is in the male line. The successor is assigned with the duties only after acquiring necessary training and learning customary laws.

Kaikariam are Tamil Brahmins. They perform duties at the temple gate. Opening and closing of temple gate at scheduled time is their responsibility. Temple gate opens in the morning and closes in the afternoon for an hour. It reopens at two pm. and finally closed at nine pm. Before final closing of the gate the Kaikariam take vigilance around. After closing the door one set of key is handed over to the office of the Joint commissioner and another set to the chief priest. Earlier the temple duty of Kaikariam was succeeded from generation to generation, from father to a son but now-a-days they are selected through interview. Earlier their duties were controlled within the group through *pali* system but nowadays duties are allotted by the temple administration. They also organise *shringar*, adornment of the deities including bathing and dressing according to different *thithi* and festivities. The Kaikarim group also looks after security of the temple. Yoshi belong to the immigrant Brahman group. Their duty is to find out *tithi*, *Nakhatra*, time and period for the worship throughout the year and make a schedule for worship. They are also responsible for timely *puja* and other related functions to be performed by the priest properly.

The *Sadhak* or Achariya is divided into two sections, each associated with a definite kind of service. One is the *Havan* group and the other group is to assist the main *pujari* at the time of *puja*. The *Havan* group of *Sadhak* (Achariya) belongs to local Tamil Brahmin. They assist *Shringar* group of Brahmin and perform *Havan* (offering an oblation to fire) during the *puja*.

The Maniar supervises all the daily activities of the temple related work. The Maniar group belongs to local group of Brahmin. They take care so that all the essential items for *puja* like fruit, milk, flower etc. should reach in time before the worship. Besides, there is O-Duar group, who are associated with the temple since early days. They sing before the mother goddess Parvati during her bed time in the night and in the morning next day to get her up from sleep. The O-duar group belongs to Tamil Saivait. The Saraiyar group is involved in arranging and preparing Naivadhya (food offerings for the god) to be offered during worship.

In Rameswaram temple different types of food items are prepared by the Parichayakar and their assistants locally known as Barkar. The food for the Gods is called *Bhoga*. The Parichayakar traditionally prepare *Bhoga* since the days of King's ruling. Now *Bhoga* menu is taken care of by the temple administration. The Parichayakar and Barkar serve their duties on rotation. Another group of temple servitor is Para. They are engaged as security workers. They look after security during worship and make the way clear from the visitors while *Bhoga* is carried from kitchen to the temple.

In the early days, altogether fifty five families were involved in the temple services including both Tamil and Maharashtrian Brahmins. Presently only twenty eight families are associated with such kind of activities. The priests, before getting responsibility of temple service, have to undergo training and to qualify for the service. At the first step they are to attend the *Agam-bidhi patshala*, a school for such specific training where they learn respective knowledge and qualify for the examination at Madurai and Kottakulam. After completion of the first step of learning they are to join Shankaracharcha Asharam and gets *Avisekam-diskha,* i.e., formal initiation to ritualistic activities. In case of Priestly services, the newly trained are to work under the senior priest for a period of one or two years as apprentices. They assist the seniors and learn the methods of offering and other activities related to worship. After completion of apprenticeship the seniors certify the juniors that they would be allowed to perform the priestly job of worship. A formal interview is conducted by the Joint-Commissioner for priesthood. In case of other posts the temple administration advertises in the local news papers accordingly and the candidates apply for the post along with their experience. The selection committee conducts interview and the panel of selected candidates is forwarded to the Sharba-sadaga group and Panchha committee; the committee approve the panel and finally send to the Chairman of the body for appointment and financial approval.

Temple Administration

Since beginning of the temple, different rulers have ruled the area and supervised the temple management. During British era, the Government also ruled over the temple administration. Till 1883, a successor of Vellala hermits was in charge of the temple; when their line of descent became extinct, the District Judge of Madurai, took over and managed the temple through a receiver. Subsequently, under Act XX of 1863 Managers were appointed by the court for some time and finally in 1912, a scheme was framed by the Sub-Judge of Ramnad under which a committee of five members was constituted for a term of five years and special representation was given to the Setupatti of Ramanathapuram and a member of the ALAR family. The scheme has since been modified and a Board of Trustees under the Madras HR and CE Act of 1959 has been managing the temple with an Executive Officer of gazetted rank, at present the Joint Commissioner HR and CE (A) Department. No employee of the temple has any vested right to any office or emoluments. After independence the Government of India took over the charge of the temple administration in the year of 1955 under the Hindu Regulation Amendment Rule.

The resource of the temple has been adversely affected by land Legislation. The income is now mainly from Tasdic allowance and produce from lands those are still under the possession of the temple, Kattalais and offering from devotees and sale proceeds of tickets for *sevas*. The average annual income is about two crores but it is hardly found sufficient to maintain the temple satisfactorily. Donation and endowments is thankfully received by the temple and all donors earn blessings of Lord Ramanatha and Devi Parvathavardhini.

In the present day, the temple administration is run by two tire system. One the Pancha committee formed of the king (Kumarran Sethupathi), Nato-Patti-Chettiyar, a representative of Chettiyars (since from the early days the Chettiyars play an important role in the history of Tamil Nadu as well as Rameswaram temple) and three renowned persons from the local area. In case of first two categories the post is hereditary and succeeded from generation to generation in the male line only. In case of the third

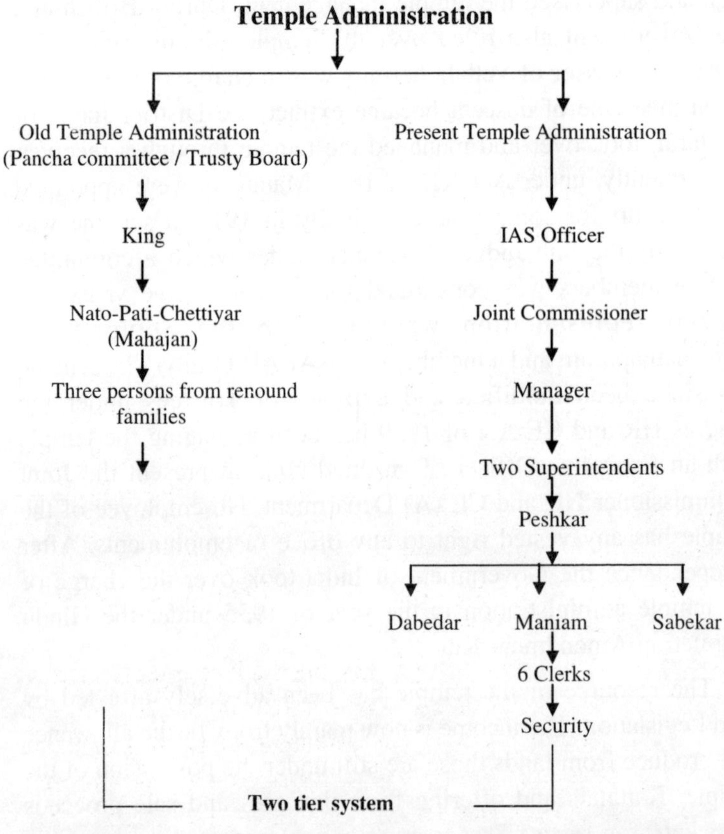

category on death of any candidate the temple administration selects the next suitable candidate from the local area. The two tier administration system is inter-linked with each others.

The other body is locally known as Temple Administration, consists of Government employees and the descendants of old temple employees. The administration is headed by an I.A.S officer appointed at Madras. The second position is occupied by the joint commissioner who sits at temple office of Rameswaram. The third position is of Manager who also sits at temple office. In the temple administration there are two superintendents of whom one comes from Government department and other is selected from descends of old temple employees. Next stratum is Peshkar; there are three categories of posts namely Dabedar, Maniam and Sabekar. In the old administrative system there used to be one assistant Peshkar but the post does not exist in present day. There are six Clarks working under the temple administration. Besides, there are temple securities. In the present day, both the Pancha committee and the temple administrative body run the temple administration work.

The temple committee maintains financial matter, daily activities of the temple, annual festival, recruitment and welfare activities. The Pancha committee looks after the activities of main body. For any activities other than the worship like new construction inside the temple premise, any programme to be performed by the temple committee, any new appointment to the temple or to arrange meetings, etc., approval from the Pancha committee is mandatory. Role of temple administrators is as follows: the Chairperson is the appointing authority to the temple; Joint commissioner supervises all the functions and daily routine work of the temple; manager maintains daily account as well as accounts of the temple properties; the Superintendent is also associated with the account maintaining system. The Dabedar looks after the worship activities of the priest and timely supply the necessary articles. Maniam supervises the duties and activities of the priest. The Sabekar maintains store of the temple and supply food materials for Bhoga according to the daily routine. The Clerks are assigned to different duties; one group sale the ticket for *Bhoga*, the other group maintains official work of the temple administration. The Security people assure security of the temple.

The temple has its own law and order system; there are definite rules and regulation for the devotees also. Besides, the administration maintains welfare activities, fairs and festivities and development activities.

Observation

The study reflects that man and religion is in a twine relationship. Man takes religious shelter for spiritual satisfaction likewise the religious power gives mental spirit to the man for continued existence. It is a common religious phenomenon all over the world. To perform religious activities, the devotees depend on the Priest; he is the link between the devotee and God. The continued interaction between the devotee and the priest over generations resulted into systematic maintenance of the records. The records maintaining system help the priest to recall the devotee's name, residential place and other information at a glance. This system also helps judicial system in drawing family history of a particular case. Such system has also developed a Guru-*Shishya* relationship and an economic chain in the society in the name of religion.

Over the passage of time, the country has witnessed different rulers and changing socio-economic-politico-religious scenario and in more recent years passing through the process of modernisation, globalisation each of which has its own impact; but in the field of religion the priests maintain religious rhythm of life in its own way. As a result, this age old knowledge system is surviving and is carried forward to next generation and the data bank is preserved for the use of future generation.

Acknowledgements

I am greatly indebted to Dr V. R. Rao, former Director-in-Charge, Anthropological Survey of India, for taking initiative and designing the project and giving me the opportunity to study this interesting subject. I express my sincere thanks to Prof K.K. Misra, Director, Anthropological Survey of India, Kolkata for his initiative in publishing this report. Prof Yogesh Atal and Prof A.C. Bhagabati offered valuable suggestions to enrich the study. I am thankful to them. I am greatly obliged to the Commissioner of Rameshwaram temple and his temple administrative machinery for their untiring support during my field investigation. I owe a special gratitude to Chief Priest of the Rameshwaram temple Mr Vital Barve and Mr Srikanth Jagannath Ekbote and his brother Mr Pramod Kumar Ekbote for their kind cooperation. With their assistance I could understand the temple administration and division of labour among the priests. I wish to thank Dr K. Chakrabarty, P.I. and Head of Office, Anthropological Survey of India, Eastern Regional Centre, Kolkata for giving me opportunity to study the Rameshwaram temple. I am also obliging those who helped me directly or indirectly to complete the report writing.

References

Amirthalingam. A. (1972) Gazetteer Unit, Revenue Department No. 6, Gandhi-Irwin Road, Egmore, Madras-8.

Temple Administration, (2006) Arulmigu Ramanathaswamy Temple Rameswaram Temple Publications.

Appendix I

The temple administration developed some rules and regulation regarding Abishegasm and Archanas (worship) to Lord Ramanatha and Goddess Sri Parvathavardhini. The devotees can offer puja from distant places also by sending money to the temple authorities. On behalf of the devotee the temple administration makes necessary arrangement to perform puja and Prasadam (the sanctified food of the god) is sent to the devotee to respective address.

Abishegam

The expenditure associated with Abishegam and Archanas:

1.	Sahasra Kalasa Abishegam	Rs 5,000.00
2.	Sahasra Sangabishegam (1008)	Rs 5,000.00
3.	Ashtothra Kalasa Abhishegam	Rs 1,000.00
4.	Rudhrabishegam	Rs 1,500.00
5.	Ubayabishegam	Rs 1,000.00
6.	Sangabishegam(108 with Neivedhyam)	Rs 1,000.00
7.	Gangabishegam (including Ganga water and Vessel)	Rs 30.00
8.	Gangabishegam Ticket fee	Rs 20.00
9.	Milk Abishegam (exclusive milk)	Rs 25.00
10.	Spadigalinga abishega Dharshan fee	Rs 15.00
11.	Rose water Abishegam (excluding Rose water)	Rs 25.00
12.	Special Entry fee Swamy sannathi	Rs 50.00
13.	Special Entry fee Ambal sannathi	Rs 10.00
14.	Kodi theertham abishegam	Rs 25.00
15.	Vibuthi abishegam	Rs 25.00

Archanas

1.	Sahasranama Archana to Sri Ramanathaswamy	Rs 200.00
2.	Sahasranama Archana to Sri Ambal	Rs 200.00
3.	Boondhi Laddu	Rs 100.00
4.	Adhirasam	Rs 100.00

5. Vadaimalai Rs 100.00
6. For other Neivedhyams- each Rs 100.00
7. Ashotothra Archna to Sri Ramanathaswamy Rs 5.00
8. Ashtothraarchana to Sri Parvathavardhini and other Sannathis Rs 5.00
9. Bathing in the Kodi Theertham and all other Therthams each person Rs 13.00

Other Tickets

1. To offer Rudhrajabam per head Rs 25.00
2. To take bath in the Lakshman Theertham Rs 01.00
3. Fee for taking Kodi Theertham in the vessel Rs 03.00

Other Pujas

1. Puja fee for five times Rs 25,000.00
2. Puja fee for one time Rs 5000.00

Puja with Decorations

1. For offering Puja to presiding Goddes with Gold Kavasam Rs 201.00
2. For offering Puja to Ramanatha with Gold Kavasam and Nagaparanam Rs 201.00

Utsavams

1. Silver Chariot Utsaam Rs 75,000.00
2. Panjamoorthy Utsavam Rs 10,000.00
3. Decorating Sri Ambal and taking round the third corridor on Golden Chariot Rs 2,000.00

Permanent Endowment

The above Abishegams will be performed regularly on a particular day out of the interest earned on the following amount and prasad will be sent.

1.	For Rudhrabishegam	Rs 15000.00
2.	For Rudhrajabam and Ganga abishegam	Rs 3,000.00
3.	For One-time Puja	Rs 7,000.00
4	Free distribution Neivedhya Prasadam	Rs 10,000.00
5.	For Gangabishegam	Rs 3,000.00
6.	Dheepa Kattalai	Rs 3,000.00
7.	Annathana Kattalai	Rs 40,000.00

Income Tax relief is available for the donations. The interested Devotees contact the Executive officer of the temple for arranging archanas and accommodation.

Appendix II

The twelve Jotirlingams are:

1. Sri Somnatheswara, Sourashtra
2. Sri Mallikarjuna, Srisailam
3. Sri Mahakaleswara, Ujjain
4. Sri Omkareswara, Amaleswaram
5. Sri vaidhyanath, Parali
6. Sri Bimasankara, Dhakini
7. Sri Nageswara, Dharugavanam
8. Sri Kasi Viswanath, Banaras
9. Sri Thriyambakeswara, Nasik
10. Sri Kedareswara, Himalayam
11. Sri Kushruneswara, Ellora
12. Rameswaram, Tamil Nadu

Priest and Devotees at Rameswaram Temple.

The Priest Listening to the Devotees at Rameswaram.

The Priest Arranging *Bhog* for Worship.

***Banshabali* (Genealogical Record) at Rameswaram.**

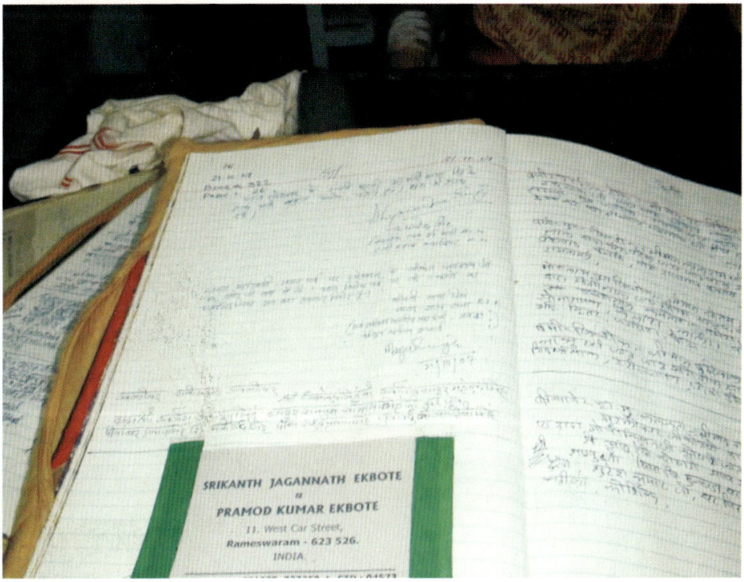

***Banshabali* Book.**

Devotees Performing Ancestral Worship at Dhanus Kutti, Rameswaram.

Performing Ancestral Worship at Dhanus Kutti, Rameswaram.

The Chief Priest and Dignitaries at Rameswaram Temple.

Index